We can easily forgive a child who is afraid of the dark; the real tragedy of life is when men are afraid of the light.
Plato (426BC-347BC)

FROM THE AUTHOR OF
MORPHEUS POSSESSED:
THE CONFLICT BETWEEN DREAM AND REALITY
AND
MORPHEUS UNCHAINED:
REMEMBRANCES OF A FUTURE DREAM

MORPHEUS' CHALLENGE

Beyond the Dreams

W. E. GUTMAN

CCB Publishing
British Columbia, Canada

Morpheus' Challenge: Beyond the Dreams

Non-fiction. Essays on life, death, and the lunatic ambivalence of the human spirit.

Copyright ©2019 by W. E. Gutman
ISBN-13 978-1-77143-381-5
First Edition

Library and Archives Canada Cataloguing in Publication
Gutman, W. E., 1937-, author
Morpheus' challenge : beyond the dreams
/ written by W. E. Gutman. -- First edition.
Issued in print and electronic formats.
ISBN 978-1-77143-381-5 (pbk.).--ISBN 978-1-77143-382-2 (pdf)
Additional cataloguing data available from Library and Archives Canada

Cover design by the author.

Cover background: Grey paper texture:
© valkot | Canstockphoto.com

This book is printed on acid-free paper.

Extreme care has been taken by the author to ensure that all information presented in this book is accurate and up to date at the time of publishing. The publisher cannot be held responsible for any errors or omissions. Additionally, neither is any liability assumed by the publisher for damages resulting from the use of the information contained herein.

Publisher: CCB Publishing
                  British Columbia, Canada
                  www.ccbpublishing.com

Also by W. E. GUTMAN

JOURNEY TO XIBALBA:
The Subversion of Human Rights in Central America
Reporter's Notebook. Non-fiction. © 2000 (out of print)

NOCTURNES — *Tales from the Dreamtime*
Fantasy fiction. © 2006

FLIGHT FROM EIN SOF
Satire. © 2009

THE INVENTOR
Historical fiction. © 2009

A PALER SHADE OF RED — *Memoirs of a Radical*
Autobiography. © 2012

ONE NIGHT IN COPAN — *Chronicles of Madness Foretold*
Tales of mystery, fantasy and horror. © 2012

ONE LAST DREAM
Screenplay. © 2012

UN DERNIER REVE (One Last Dream)
Screenplay (French version). © 2012

ALL ABOUT EARTHLINGS: *The Irreverent Musings*
of an Extraterrestrial Envoy - Dystopia, parody © 2015

MORPHEUS POSSESSED:
The Conflict Between Dream and Reality
Essay. © 2015

MORPHEUS UNCHAINED:
Remembrances of a Future Dream
Essay. © 2016

Contents

War is just a racket. Only a small inside group knows what it is about. It is conducted for the benefit of the very few at the expense of the masses.
Gen. Smedley Butler, U. S. Marine Corps
(1881-1940)

Human decency is not derived from religion.
It precedes it.
Christopher Hitchens (1949-2011)

*The whole of world history often seems to me
nothing more than a picture book which portrays
humanity's most powerful and senseless desire –
the desire to forget.*
Hermann Hesse (1877-1962)

WHEN TIME STANDS STILL

A funny thing happened shortly before dawn as I stirred from a dream-laden torpor: Time stood still. If no one is there to traverse it, when the instruments that mark its passage and lend it meaning have stopped (or been obliterated, as many of my dreams foretell), time suspends its flight. It can then be rewound and replayed frame by frame like a stream of near-death mirages. What we regard as dreams, often dismissed as idle fancies, are, in fact, stray pages torn out pell-mell from an inexhaustible and unexpurgated collection of illuminated conversations with our inner self.

Aristotle said that when men dream, something in their consciousness declares that what then presents itself to them is but a dream. It can also be said that when they dream, something in their subconscious asserts that what they see is nothing less than reality at its most grotesque. That's one way of easing the pangs of remorse, of soothing a tainted conscience. As we return to our physical reality, the vivid spectacles to which we were treated disintegrate and disperse like clouds on a windy day.

I was still in a state of numbing languor when the past burst in like a purulent abscess, regurgitating its odious excretions and bringing up with them foretastes of a future that can be simultaneously inferred and glimpsed with great clarity and alarm because it unfailingly mimics every day, hour, minute, and second of recorded time. Past is prelude. The present is the future's compliant co-conspirator.

It was during this temporal intermission that a scene of chaos and madness and despair that I knew would echo without respite till the end of days flashed before my eyes. I first relived my birth in a Paris private clinic where chic ladies have their babies— or abort them. The procedure nearly killed my mother. I then witnessed the German occupation — I vividly remember seeing the invading troops march on the Champs Élysées as people wept. I re-lived my father's arrest by the Gestapo, his miraculous getaway, a saga of endurance and courage that spared us deportation to the Nazi death camps where his entire family perished but did not free us from the bondage of an endlessly nomadic existence.

I then glimpsed a mass of humanity, a formless accretion of flesh and bone and sinew slog across viscous streams of time adjourned and through the horrors and ecstasies of brute existence as they crossed paths, mingled, and thronged about, heroes and villains, poltroons and paladins, liars and truth-telling whistle-blowers, unchaste men of God and noble here-tics, ruthless warriors and conscientious objec-tors, arms merchants and money-lenders, landlords and the tenants they fleece, politi-cians and the citizens they dupe, lawmakers and the private interests to which they are beholden.

What I observed in a nanosecond of excru-ciating lucidity were fast-motion flashbacks from a familiar choreography of erratic, sense-less, often demented agitation followed by moments of inertia during which millions suffered and died. Abel at the hand of his brother Cain. Jews and Moslems by crusading marauders. Cathars by papal decree. Yet more Jews and Muslims during the "Holy" Inquisition. Native Americans by bearded men wielding a cross in one hand and a sword in the other. The slave trade. Wars of "liberation;" wars of conquest and domination. That was just the beginning. Torn between reality and idealization, between cynicism and senseless hope, trapped in alternating states of boredom and freneticism, nameless, faceless souls acted out an obscure imitation of life in which every scene is a contest between good and evil, between rivalry and teamwork, betrayal and loyalty, dishonesty and righteousness, tyranny and emancipation, hate and love, finite life and inescapable death--a cinéma vérité in which are exposed the murky nature of statecraft, the perfidy of politics, and the duplicity of religion. Unfolding before me, the visions and trances surged and revealed themselves at once touching and obscene, infuriating and dispiriting. They lingered in my mind's eyes long after I opened them and reentered the world of madness and incongruity into which I was born and lived, a world that even nightmares cannot envision or replicate. Reality eclipses and outperforms the most imaginative novel, the most monstrous dream. This is why I no longer read novels. This is perhaps why we dream.

◆

As he released me from his embrace and retreated to the spectral shadows of his mother Night's abode, I thought I heard Morpheus whisper in my ear:

"In my arms men dream," he said. "It is when I surrender them to their wits that they hallucinate, that the delirium begins, that their lusts, phobias, and fixations are in full view. Every day the sun exhausts titanic amounts of energy that can never be rekindled. It is doomed to a fiery death. Every day, mankind wastes energy equivalent to 400,000 Hiroshima bombs. Every night are relived the secret cravings that devour men by day and which, if sated, can never be expunged. I suspect many live exemplary lives not because they are virtuous but because they lack the courage, the opportunity, or the faculty to err. The repentant man is more honorable than the man who never sins. Alas, both are in very short supply. Being the catalyst of their fertile meanderings,

5

I bring them messages and prophecies from the gods through the medium of dreams. I am the embodiment of abstract ideas but I cannot tell them what to dream. I can only lure them to sleep and draw faint outlines of the incongruities that their altered minds concoct. You, on the other hand, have gone beyond the dreams, filled in the blanks, exposed the dreamers. You have navigated the stormy seas that separate phantasm from perceived reality; you regaled us with your own irreverent nocturnal emissions. You once wrote—and I quote:

> *The status quo is a perpetual-motion nightmare from which we must awaken, or it will extinguish our dreams. We keep looking at ourselves in the cosmos' endless void and finding nothing but billions of sepulchers in which our fantasies are entombed. There is no one else out there. Humankind is a unique and unrepeatable biological eccentricity forever destined to ponder the enigma of its absurd existence. The mission of sane men is not to reach for the stars but to strive toward refinement through reformation. We shall never ascend to the Dreamdom unless we make a left turn, arm the powerless, infuriate the moneyed elites, crush the mighty, and agitate, agitate, agitate. There*

can be no meaningful revolution without a revolution.

"This is my challenge and my promise," Morpheus added. "Wake up and take us back to the Stygian depths where the dreams are spawned. Remind us again of the paradoxes, the aberrations, the deceptions, and the monstrosities that define man and mark the human condition. And I shall grant the innocent and the righteous *ataraxia*. That's what we ancient Greeks call everlasting inner peace: the conscious ability to rise above the fear, anger, sadness, and stresses that plague us outside the dream."

JOURNALISM AT THE CROSSROADS

Journalism is the first draft of history. Indelible renderings of the human drama are seized then frozen in time on the printed page and on the airwaves. Delivered "as is," facts should discourage revisionists from tampering with the truth. Alas, for many, fact has become calumny, reality a foe, truth an affront. For those whose only loyalty is to the truth, it's a lonely, dangerous world.

The price for such devotion is often steep and those who are willing to pay for it never lack enemies. Are some journalists hurtling down the rabbit hole of evasion, stonewalling, and conscious self-censorship? Who speaks for those who can't speak freely?

To the enemies of truth, newsmen make appetizing quarries. If our exposés or commentaries are too graphic, irreverent, or too close for comfort, we're accused of needlessly giving our audiences palpitations. No matter what we report, we're sure to be reviled by someone along the way.

Of course, readers are not a homogeneous lot. They come in sundry stripes, hues, and biases. Mercifully many seek to be informed. Most possess the mental elasticity to judge news reports or opinion pieces on their own merits. It is to them that scrupulous journalists devote their columns and newscasts. Some readers, hasty or inattentive like disoriented butterflies, take things out of context. They misconstrue. They see conspiracy in syntax. They scrutinize and dissect every utterance as if it concealed some subversive codded message. They can't see the sentence from the words. Some even advocate censorship — voluntary or state-imposed. They are so jarred by the truth that they want it suppressed, obliterated, reduced to ashes ... along with those who unearth it.

This may explain why some media outlets

and networks, to survive, rhapsodize the irrelevant, beat around the bush, and shy away
from the pressing issues of the day. Not all
journalists rush in where angels fear to tread.
Some are daunted by the naked truth. Others
just want to keep their jobs.

Political correctness (the sacrifice of truth
at the altar of hypocrisy) keeps readers, view-
ers, and especially advertisers happy. Unlike
open scandal, which peaks in an orgy of finger-pointing and vitriol, then dies, self-
censorship leaves a trail of speculations and a
scent of putrefaction. It's bad enough when
governments hide behind a wall of secrecy
and lies; it's worse when some members of the
Fourth Estate, the conscience of a free society,
sheepishly corrupt their mission by coddling
the powers that be, by colluding to keep the
public in the fog of ignorance. It is the height
of obscenity when governments urge the media to look the other way and threaten to gag
them if they refuse.

Despite opinions to the contrary, journalists do not get paid to generate solutions for
the problems they cite. Our job is to uncover,
observe, and report. Solutions can only be ex-
tracted from the problems themselves. It is up
to those who create them to solve them.

What emerges from some critics' taunts is the appalling suggestion that baring verifiable facts, telling irrefutable truths, is an act of disloyalty. A free, independent press is the bedrock of democracy. Analytical criticism is not unpatriotic. It's a fundamental right, an obligation, and an exercise in rational citizenship. Silence is the real villain and those who keep silent are the real traitors, the purveyors of fake news, the enemies of the people. The truth is immutable.

IN PURSUIT OF UTOPIA

Several years ago, the late editor-in-chief of a leading West-Indian newspaper told me, off the record:

"Come now, you don't expect us to survive on sugar cane, rum, nutmeg, and an occasional goodwill visit by one of the royals, can you? We've got to put on our affable, soft-spoken, 'happy native' faces. That's what keeps tourists coming. They see neither the grinding poverty that festers in the shadow of classy 'all-inclusive' resorts, nor do they hear the murmurs of discontent that echo in the back streets and the shanties. Seduced by paradise, the tourists return. They feed our national ego, keep our flag unfurled, and they unwittingly or quite uncaringly hold us in a state of economic servitude from which only a privileged few can escape."

Fast forward. Grenada, August 2012. Sunset had hushed the ebbing echoes of Carnival. The drums were now silent and people, young and old, some who toil from dawn until late into the night to make ends meet, lumbered home, a mixture of fading ecstasy and blissful exhaustion etched upon their faces. I caught up with a few stragglers on the dimming streets of St. George's.

"Tell me what it means to be West Indian," I asked. All had a presence about them, a quiet air of self-worth that spoke volumes of their struggles, expectations, and disappointments. Some mentioned a "failed revolution" that was to bring needed reforms and was "usurped by the moneyed elite with the connivance of a foreign power." They were no doubt referring to the United States.

Others, who had not been born or were too young to remember the events that rocked the island nation more than three decades ago, hinted at an "undercurrent of pessimism" now sweeping Grenadian society, a "disconnect" between the people and the government, and "an abyss" separating the idle rich and working class.

A high school senior spoke of the future with trepidation. "Where do I go from here? Where are the jobs? If I stay, opportunities are scant. If I go abroad and return with a degree, opportunities are nil. I must either join the growing West Indian diaspora or settle for some menial job in the service industry right here at home."

Later that evening, dining at a trendy seaside eatery, I broke bread with a fellow newsman who spoke of the painful tradeoffs tourism imposes on developing countries. With annual revenues exceeding $3 billion, he said, the economic impact of tourism is second only to that of the weapons industry.

"If tourism is good for tourists and the businesses that cater to them," I asked, "how good is it for host nations?"

"Tourism has made some people immensely rich," he conceded. "But it has also brought about very stark and painful consequences. Developers fill in swamps and mangroves, destroy coral reefs, gouge beaches to create docks and marinas, causing a chain reaction that hurts fishing, reduces the supply of fresh water for irrigation, and shrinks the land base. Locals are relegated to infertile lands or degraded urban settings while the environment and artificial 'cultures' are recreated atop the ruins of the real thing. Tourism relies on powerful and often unprincipled marketing strategies."

Quite disingenuously, promoters claim that tourism is the only way for developing nations to erect a social and economic Utopia. History is full of dreamers who sought to create what they imagined to be a perfect world — generally without the world's consent and more often than not at its detriment. Take the growing fleet of multi-story cruise ships. Pollution from these behemoths of the sea is immense, despite claims that newer vessels are clean and green. Princess Cruises was fined $40 million for polluting oceans since 2005. All ships are powered by heavy petroleum, a sludgy tar-like fuel that produces noxious fumes that harm not only passengers but all those in the vicinity of the ship, while greatly accelerating climate change. Estimates put the average daily fuel usage of each of these ships at 150 tons of fuel, which releases as much particulate matter into the air as about 1 million automobiles each day! Cruise ships also devastate oceans when they dump raw sewage from their passengers. A 2014 study by the non-governmental environmental agency, Friends of the Earth, estimated that the entire industry dumps over 1 billion gallons of sewage yearly. In less affluent countries that are popular as cruise ship destinations, however, residents will likely suffer more when cruise ships that failed to improve their pollution levels dock in areas reliant on tourism dollars.

♦

It is no surprise that, in 2011, at the behest of then Governor Rick Scott, officials of Florida's Dept. of Environmental Protection, the agency in charge of setting conservation policy and enforcing environmental laws, issued directives forbidding employees from using terms such as "climate change," "global warming," "sustainability," or "sea-level rise," with the latter to be referred to as *"nuisance flooding."* Nuisance flooding from tropical cyclones is responsible for more than half of all fatalities; material damage from rising sea levels is nearly impossible to quantify. Florida, home base for many Caribbean- Mexico- and Central

America-bound cruise liners, has been described as "uniquely vulnerable to sea-level rise" and is said to be "under an imminent threat of increased inland flooding due to climate change."

No wonder TV meteorologists I contacted, asking them why they did not attribute unusual or violent weather patterns to man-made pollution refused to answer me. The topic is political poison. If they admitted that much, factories would have to be shut down, cruise ships would have to be kept at bay, thus resulting in multibillion dollar losses. Money *uber alles!* This is the freaking Globo-fascism I keep talking about. Here's the paradox: Hitler, Stalin, and Mao killed several million people and were rightfully denounced as monsters. Trans-national companies destroy the very possibility of life on Earth—it is nothing short of an omnicide, yet no one seems to care, least of all those who profit from their own criminal enterprises.

◆

Tourism (like political partisanship) promotes and subsidizes biased, sometimes deceptive journalism. It rewards writers who focus on

the positive and steer clear of critical analysis.
[I recall a travelogue hosted by Samantha
Brown in which, while focusing on the charming and relatively safe village of Copán, site of
important pre-Columbian ruins, said not a
word about Honduras, for many years the
most violent and crime-ridden country in Central America.] Travel brochures weave "magi-
cal dreams of paradise" in countries where
paradise is more candy for the eye than food
for the belly or social justice for the underdog.
Ads gloss over the economic, environmental,
and social problems rife in the areas they
promote. Travel agents, a dying breed, conspire by recommending destinations they
know little about. Amateur travel writers, often more interested in self-promotion or curry-
ing favor with the cruise lines, hotels, and res-
taurants they patronize, usually distort the
truth or ignore it altogether. Last, tourists unwittingly abet human rights abuses by ignoring corrupt or oppressive governments that
salivate at the almighty dollar.

In the abstract, well planned, wisely fund-
ed, skillfully nurtured, and lovingly managed,
tourism—as the much vaunted "model cities"
—can become a paradigm for steady socio-
economic and cultural self-renewal. In the

hands of buccaneers, opportunity degenerates into opportunism and the Utopian dream turns to dystopian nightmare. Karl Popper warned that Utopia tends toward despotism. Mario Vargas Llosa added that the idea of a perfect society is the trademark of monsters. "When you want paradise, you first generate extraordinary idealism. You then produce hell." Vargas was referring to the tyranny of inflexible dogmas – ultra-nationalism and the fanciful promise of heaven made by religion. But he was also guarding against the notion that castles in the sky can be erected without risk or counter-intuitive consequences.

Utopia? In countries unable to provide for their most vulnerable citizens? Countries where a small moneyed elite reigns supreme over masses enfeebled by penury and shrinking opportunities? Countries that depend almost entirely on tourism for their survival? Countries that ad-lib their politics and govern without a blueprint for the future? Will these Utopias be paved with gold or will shanty-towns teeming with human chaff mushroom on the fringes of luxury hotels and hilltop villas?

Utopia is a Greek word. It means "no place; nowhere." It exists only in the minds of

misguided do-gooders, mystics, and charlatans. Model states? Models of what? Are they,
like Thomas More's fantastical locale, superla-
tive habitats ruled by the people and free from
interference by a malevolent "deep state"? Or,
more likely, will they turn out to be places of
privilege for the well-to-do and cash cows for
greedy investors and speculators—domestic
and foreign? After all, wasn't it Thomas More
who declared in 1516 in his *Utopia*, that *"People
always talk about the public interest, but all
they really care about is themselves and private
property."*?

THE TOXIC NORMALCY OF CORRUPTION

Corruptibility is the mother of all vices. Without it, we'd live in a fiction-like world of virtue, unconditional love, and justice. It is as powerful an impulse as the reproductive urge or the survival instinct. Because we're human, we're all susceptible to its siren call. Self-delusion, the perversion of reality as a hedge against the sobering effect of reason, is its commonest incarnation. People who search for (or believe they've found) paradise are the most deluded but their fantasies are usually short-lived and harmless—except for those they try to inoculate against reality.

Also predisposed toward corruptibility are those whose conduct can be manipulated. Pretending to be what our parents, teachers, spiritual leaders, employers, and the ruling class expect from us can result in small rewards or, at the very least, protect us from censure, or punishment. And then there are those who can be corrupted by money and will do anything for it—lie, cheat, betray, torture, and even kill. In some countries, particularly among the poorest (but by no means confined to them) corruption is the bedrock in which governance and commerce are fused and anchored. It's become a habitual, ritualized, institutionalized reflex. It's part of the social fabric. People have become so inured to it from youth that they no longer recognize it for what it really is: the process of decay by which nations eventually collapse.

There is a direct correlation between how people are empowered in their societies and their leaders' propensity to circumvent or violate basic covenants, to lie, to be suborned and engage in the wholesale sellout of their citizens. Where people have an unimpeded voice and where a lively civil culture thrives, those in authority cannot escape public scrutiny, less yet evade public condemnation.

In contrast, in crypto-monocracies such as those found in Central America, where I spent twelve years on assignment, where wealth and political power are confined to a small, wealthy, all-powerful oligarchy, people have a nominal voice but no clout, especially where their vital interests — life, liberty, and the pursuit of happiness — are curtailed and further compromised by endemic crime, violence, and the appalling indifference of their leaders. *El Querido Pueblo* just doesn't count. Those who protest are either ignored, their grievances lost in the murky corridors of officialdom, or they risk surveillance, harassment, even assassination.

"We've been reduced to turning our heads and looking the other way," a Honduran judge told me on condition of anonymity. "We overlook corruption, we tacitly condone it because doing otherwise will have grave consequences. To be perceived as honest or as a champion of the little guy is to stand out. Defenders of just causes don't die of old age."

There are other dynamics that prevent people from listening to their conscience. One of them is the stupefying realization that their elected officials, given their own venality and the tangled cabals in which they engage—

often in cahoots with criminal elements — are so inextricably ensnared in shady activities that they would be unable to fix the problems they created or abetted, even if they tried.

There are two types of corruption: corruption of opportunity and corruption of necessity. The former is instinctive. It will thrive as long as humans rule the planet. The latter occurs when, reduced to their primal state and unable to survive by any other means, people are forced to break the law. Their synchronism is not coincidental. The poorer the nation, the wealthier the governing elite, the more capital is concentrated in fewer hands, the greater the opportunity by the leaders and necessity by the led to do evil. Corruption does not occur in a vacuum. It is a system of values and behaviors that straddles the public and private domain: the corruptible always have a corrupter to turn to.

Any profound and lasting remedy calls for cultural and attitudinal transformations, as well as a radical shakeup of the structures and substructures most vulnerable to corruptibility. It was with both surprise and elation that I learned that several police precincts in Guatemala had fired every cop on the beat, dismissed all rookies, and hired and trained new cadres whose character, moral fiber, and susceptibility to corruption were painstakingly scrutinized. The result: a swift and significant drop in police misconduct and a higher rate of arrests and convictions of narcotraffickers and other criminals.

Guatemala's neighbors might be well served to take notice. A good start might be to sack every politician, from the president on down, purging all military personnel trained by the U.S. Army School of the Americas, and reassigning every member of the constabulary to the Sanitation Corps.

LIBERTARIANISM:
CRANK IDEAL OR CLEVER PLOY?

Libertarianism is a sloppily coined word and deceptively marketed ideology that hallows "the right of free choice." It comes in two flavors. One masks the stench of "inherent rights" that ignore societal obligations and responsibilities. The other spices up "individual rights" with a heady bouquet of causal assumptions about what leads to freedom and productivity.

Those who call themselves Libertarians muddle these elements, sometimes deliberately, more often out of ignorance or exasperation with real or perceived existential threats. The

18th century antiroyalist writers who inspired France and a nascent United States, advocated against despotism, not legitimate governance. Wittingly or unwittingly, ostensible Libertarian "rights" work against the greater good of all.

This is the philosophical side of the debate. Reality casts an uglier light.

Libertarianism can be likened to a form of "Marxism of the Right." Neoconservatives, with their own brand of anarchic fetishism, find an attractive political refuge in Libertarianism. It lends them a fake aura of tolerance and idealism. In fact, they believe that individual freedom should be the sole barometer of moral values, that it endows them with the clear conscience to do things that democratic nations rebuke, like sedition, secessionism, and the evasion of legitimate government oversight. It favors the imposition of a formula for the application of capitalist norms on the whole of society. As such, Libertarianism is nothing more than a seductive fallacy structurally incapable of evolving a model of how to use freedom justly. Its root dogma, that "all free choices are equal," is a theory it cannot discard without admitting that there are other virtues beside freedom.

If Marxism can be viewed as the delusion that one can run society purely on altruism and collectivism, Libertarianism is the mirror-image myth that one can run it purely on self-ishness, laissez-faire, and isolationism. Like Marxism, Libertarianism offers the fraudulent intellectual security of a complete *a priori* account of the political good without the effort of empirical investigation. Like Marxism, it aspires, overtly or covertly, to reduce social life to economics. And like Marxism, it has its historical fantasies and a genius for making its followers feel like a "Chosen People" exempted from the ethical rules that guide the majority.

Libertarians utter simplistic, if rousing catchphrases, "We love freedom; we abhor tyranny," that are not reflected in their political programs. Even when they define Libertarianism, the characterization is neither accurate nor honest. They claim that their system would produce desirable "results." Arguing from results is not enough to justify a political philosophy. The attitude of fascists, many who call themselves Libertarians, was lampooned in a famous one-liner: "Mussolini cleaned up the bordellos and made trains run on time." He did. He then dropped the pretense of democracy, created a police state, then instituted a one-party dictatorship.

Libertarians favor the deregulation and full privatization of the economy; this is typically where their instrumental claims are made. They demand that individuals accept the outcome of market forces. They legitimize economic injustice by refusing to see it as a coercive influence. Not unlike fundamentalist Christians, they exploit the political process to penetrate it and ram through faith-based agendas that conceal dangerous attitudes and objectives: "Capitalism is noble." "Worker activism and unions are evil." "The poor are pampered good-for-nothing freeloaders who deserve their fate." "Equal rights is a code word for socialism…" This philosophy, if one can call it that, is largely embodied in and drawn from Ayn Rand's objectivist tirades and Jefferson Davis' seething racism. Both Rand and Davis are the darlings of neo-cons and modern anti-abolitionists. Rand exalted egoism; she called it a "virtue." Davis referred to slavery as that "peculiar institution… the steppingstone for the Negro to become perfect."

Libertarianism is a mindset adopted by a broad spectrum of rigid — not freethinking —

individuals who clamor for "states' rights" but would merrily curtail or abolish the freedoms of those who disagree with them. CEOs of industries that discharge toxic wastes into the air, oceans, rivers, and lakes also call themselves Libertarians, as do those who would flood the country with assault weapons because an archaic and ill-worded 1791 codicil gives them that right and because they favor a "free-market" economy ... but would criminalize stem-cell research, pot-smoking, sex-sex marriage, and abortion because of their high moral convictions... but would cheer when a felon fries on the electric chair or squirms in pain as a cocktail of lethal drugs courses through his body.

Of course, Libertarianism is a word that invokes stirring values. In truth, the concept has been corrupted by profiteers and political mutineers to conceal an agenda of unfettered capitalism and religious orthodoxy. Its most ardent advocates have traded white hoods for tea bags.

On all these counts, Libertarianism simply doesn't stack up. Once people recognize it for what it truly is, expect them to toss it out as a failure and a moral mess apt to pollute and disfigure society.

INTELLIGENT DESIGN: DEFECTIVE PRODUCT

Unable to shore up the claims of creationist "science" with empirical evidence, anti-Darwinists raring to inject creationism into society's collective psyche cooked up a new slogan—"Intelligent Design"—the unproven assertion that the universe, the living things that call it home, and the unceasing upheavals they endure are the handiwork of an all-knowing, albeit paranormal cause or agent, not a freehand process such as natural selection (evolution) and the chance results of coincidence and unpredictability.

In public, most ID advocates assert that they are searching for evidence of sentient intent in nature, without regard to who or what the "designer" might be. In private, however, all unambiguously insist that the designer is the Christian God. [Note the accent on Christian. Forget the Yahweh the Jews invented nearly six thousand years before the Christian Era and the Judeo-Christian deity the Muslims adopted and renamed Allah in the 6th century].

Taken to its incongruous extremes, ID could one day be called to explain that things fall not because gravity acts upon them, but because a higher intelligence consciously and deliberately push them downward. Airplanes fall from the sky, they will argue, building collapse and empires rise and fall because these events are preordained by some inscrutable force. They do not possess the mental elasticity to concede that technology cannot exist without the potential for accidents: The invention of the locomotive also contained the invention of derailment, the airplane — of system or human failure, the stock market — of a crash. The more vicious among them will claim that these misfortunes are in fact the result of wrathful divine retribution. A large array of phenomena are already similarly attributed to ID — from wars waged in "God's" name to hunger, disease, earthquakes, cyclones, and tsunamis.

Intelligence is variously defined as "mental acuteness," the "skilled use of reason and application of knowledge," and the "ability to think abstractly" (including the capacity to envision the consequences of one's action). ID presupposes two reciprocal attributes: The existence of a gifted (if unknowable) draftsman and an exceptional blueprint from which a useful and efficient prototype can be rendered. Such inquiry-stifling premise unavoidably raises questions that, so far, ID has been unable or unwilling to explore.

Moreover, if, as *deism*, the spineless happy medium between tentative faith and unwavering atheism claims that God exists as a spontaneous First Cause ultimately responsible for the creation of the universe, but does not interfere directly with the created world … what's the point? So I ask:

What is *intelligent* about a creature that kills for pleasure and persistently breeds to extinction? What mental acuity is displayed by corruptible beings who cling to rival and inflexible doctrines. What common sense is at play among mortals shaped by greed and addicted to violence? Why are we susceptible to pain and defenseless against the fury of natural disasters that ID contends are wrought against us for "mysterious reasons" by some capricious supernatural force? What knowledge is skillfully harnessed by entities incapable or brutishly unwilling to learn from their mistakes?

What degree of intelligence can be ascribed to a "maker" who inflicts or tolerates atrocities for "the good that comes from them?" What cunning and irreducible creator orchestrates without apparent aim — or turns a blind eye to — the paroxysms that convulse his realm? What abstract reasoning inspires a "grand architect" to remain unmoved by sorrow and calamity and the ceaseless suffering of his own blueprint? What justifies such dispassion, such apathy? What superior wisdom endows itself with professed kindness and allows itself to be perceived as possessing equal doses of benevolence and evil, munificence and heartlessness, genius and folly, as circumstances dictate?

What clever inventor arms himself with an ego, gives himself a name by which others will know him in silent awe, and proclaims himself perfect and unerring while their sobs are never heard as they weep and suffer and die forgotten because pain, by some outlandish pretext, is the pathway to salvation? What supreme entity is this, whose ear is inattentive and whose breast is unfaithful to the throngs that call on him and seek his succor?

What Alpha and Omega unleashes scourges that threaten, enfeeble, and often destroy the masterwork? What cruel and invisible despot decrees that his subjects will speak words not their own, that they will blindly obey the injunctions of his self-anointed envoys, tremble at their admonitions, mouth off supplications and jeremiads and recite words of indebtedness an veneration, all repeated ad nauseam, day after day to a "God" that never shows his face, never bares his soul, never sheds a tear, never says he's sorry, a "God" who grants life and, with it, the fear of death? But "God" upon whom some turn for comfort, whose indulgence they seek for their trespasses, and whose wrath they invoke against their enemies, turns a stone visage to human misery and a deaf ear to our most heart-rending cries.

Until irrevocable proof of "Intelligent Design" is put forth—I'm not holding my breath—the concept will more likely be viewed as a clever stratagem cooked up by a new generation of hypocrites and charlatans who hijack and exploit hopelessly bewildered spirits and subvert them with falsehoods that only blind fealty can ever legitimize. ID is not only an alternate theory explaining the advent of "God's" most defective creation. It's a dangerous eccentricity concocted to exact faith by psychological extortion.

When people need to believe in something, they cease to think.

As for me, I am never more certain of my origins than when I look into the soulful eyes of a great ape. I find comfort and a sense of innocence—long since lost—in this ongoing genesis. It is when I look at myself and examine my fellow Homo sapiens that I worry about the future of the human race. This is one faulty product that can never be recalled or repaired.

WHEN SILENCE SCREAMS

For independent journalists, a breed apart known for their irreverence and persistence, silence is one loud telltale shriek. "Silence is a scoop," I was taught in journalism school, "silence is evidence of collusion or worse. When you hear nothing but the hush of obscurantism — opposition to the increase and spread of knowledge — you have a cover-up. Your job is to pull down the covers."

Unlike an open scandal, which peaks in an orgy of finger-pointing, then dies, silence leaves a trail of speculations and a scent of putrefaction. It's bad enough when elected officials hide behind a wall of secrecy; it's infinitely worse when the press, the conscience of a free society, abdicates its mission and colludes with politicians — or worse, with advertisers — to keep readers marginally informed or misinformed.

I was reminded of the lengths to which the press will go to sugarcoat or suppress certain facts as I watched "The Panama Deception" the other night while General Manuel Noriega was being flown to France to face the same bogus charges that cost him twenty years in U.S. custody.

The Academy Award-winning documentary chronicles the largely untold story of the December 1989 U.S. invasion of Panama. It analyzes the events that led to it, vividly illustrating the use of excessive force, the enormity of the death toll and devastation. The film leaves no doubt as to why this widely condemned "police action" took place, namely to silence Noriega, a CIA asset privy to a tangled web of American dirty tricks while offering a view of the invasion that differs significantly from official doublespeak and laundered media reports. It also tells how the U.S. government and mainstream dailies suppressed details about this operation or buried government-fed redacted snippets of information in their back pages.

"If journalists would only mind their damn business," some politicos grumbled. Alas, many did—and still do today. If politicians are in the business of being reelected, journalists are in the business of surviving.

Are the media slothful or too timid to point fingers or ask discomfiting questions? Or do the lies they will be forced to spread discourage them from digging for the truth?

Manuel Noriega's extradition to France, where he faced drug-related charges, refocused attention on why he became such a threat to the U.S. government and why the U.S. went to such lengths to silence him. His case also serves as a reminder of the U.S. policy of direct and indirect intervention that bedeviled Central America for decades.

Yes, Noriega is a thug.[1] But for many years he was America's thug until—like Saddam Hussein ("Our Man in Baghdad,") and other thugs the U.S. coddled—he turned on his masters. Trained at the sinister U.S. Army School of the Americas [since rechristened the Western Hemisphere Institute for Security Cooperation] also known as the "School of Assas-

---

[1] Noriega died in Panama City on May 29, 2017.

sins," Noriega became a valued CIA operative. He worked for the "Company" and for the less-than-virtuous U.S. Drug Enforcement Administration. Government documents submitted to the Miami court at his pretrial hearings in 1991 confirm that Noriega was paid about a quarter million dollars for "services rendered." He may have been paid considerably more under the table.

Noriega knew too much. He was America's ears during the "Dirty War" that engulfed El Salvador, Guatemala, Honduras, Nicaragua, and Panama. He served as liaison between then vice president George H. W. Bush and Fidel Castro in the 1980s and had met with Bush, a former CIA director, on at least two occasions. The jury at Noriega's trial never heard a word of this. Nor did it hear about his contacts with Oliver North, John Poindexter, CIA chief William Casey, and other key figures in the Reagan and Bush administration who connived in the supply of arms to Nicaragua's Contra rebels paid for with narco-dollars. Noriega had verifiable proof of U.S. complicity in politically-motivated drug-trafficking schemes. But none was entered into evidence. The U.S. rejected the Panamanian government's request that he be returned to

Panama to face a trial. In Panama, Noriega would have been free to spill the beans. And for many powerful men in Washington, some still alive and still pulling strings, that prospect was too much to bear.

The outcome of Noriega's trial, like the unprovoked 1989 invasion of Panama, was never in doubt. Noriega was railroaded in a kangaroo court bent on vengeance. It was show trial, a warning to others to clam up. It was a plot to whitewash decades of illicit meddling in the Isthmus. It was an unmistakable show of raw American muscle. The world would soon be treated to more frightening examples. And it was yet another proof that in America, if something happens but no one sees it, it didn't happen.

LIBERATION THEOLOGY SHACKLED

In *"The Failing Church,"* published in 2013 in the now defunct Honduras Weekly, Canadian journalist Paul Willcocks correctly identified the noxious effect of doctrinal orthodoxy on the lives of the flock. His coherent if somber assessment should serve as a warning against the tyranny of inflexible canons and blind obedience to absurd diktats. Of course, newsmen don't live by fact alone. Fact should always be the backbone of a story that can be bolstered by the cardinal "who," "what," "where," "when," and "how." But there is a latticework of nerve and sinew and flesh — the "why" or "why not" of an event or issue — that begs to be dissected and bared because such autopsy helps advance the cause of truth.

Bringing into focus the shadowy forces and peripheral influences that shape history, stirring the slime that percolates beneath actuality, is the sole duty of honest journalism. But doing so invites charges of muckraking, rabble-rousing, and radicalism [we have since been accused of hawking "fake news" and being "enemies of the people], labels that "mainstream" journalists, to the detriment of the Fourth Estate, work hard not to earn. Such timidity, driven by tacit covenants with, or pressure from, the government — not scruples — often leads to selective coverage and results in partial or hasty inferences slanted to conform to the prevailing attitudes of the moment. In this climate of coerced "political correctness," intemperate nationalism and religious fervor, this faint-heartedness also tends to corrupt the newsman.

Working in Central America would offer me unusual opportunities to break some taboos, (exposing U.S. criminal activities in the Isthmus), and to defy the standards of sanctioned journalism (ignoring my editors' injunctions to lay off certain subjects), sometimes at great peril. I'd long resolved to serve no master. I would neither pay lip service to Amerika's propagandists nor would I obey the conditions imposed by some of the papers for which I freelanced. In time, emboldened by the acrimony that my renderings inspired, seduced by the effect they had on readers in the Isthmus and the U.S., I would take one some of history's sinister sideshows. One was the incestuous relationship between the Church and political power structures, that grotesque symbiosis during which religion and politics intersect, merge, and feed on each other. The other was the destabilizing consequences of U.S. military adventurism in the region. The perfidious war waged by the Vatican against Liberation Theology and the wasteland of death and destruction left by alumni of the U.S. Army School of the Americas would offer me additional targets.

In appointing arch-conservative Bishop Fernando Saenz Lacalle to succeed slain Salvadoran Archbishop Oscar Romero, Pope John Paul II, then on a whirlwind tour of El Salvador, Guatemala, Nicaragua, and Venezuela, struck hard at the Theology of Liberation, the oxygen-rich doctrine—a synthesis of Christian theology and Marxist socio-economic strategies that emphasizes the political liberation for oppressed peoples — that has redefined and, for the poor and voiceless, enlivened Roman Catholicism in Latin America for more than half a century.

The roots of Liberation Theology are found in the prophetic tradition of evangelists and missionaries in early colonial Latin America — clerics who questioned the Church's elitism and who denounced the way indigenous people and the poor were being treated. Antonio de Montesinos (1480-1540), Bartolomé de las Casas (1484-1566), and Antonio Vieira (1608-1697) were some of the men who inspired the social and ecclesiastic dynamism that would later emerge in the pastoral ministry of Liberation Theology.

It was in the 1960s that an invigorating breeze wafted through the churches. They began to take their social mission seriously. Lay persons went to work among the poor. Charismatic bishops and priests called for progress and innovation. The work of these dedicated Christians, was sustained scripturally by the French theology of earthly realities, among them the integral humanism of Teilhard de Chardin (1881-1955), a Jesuit whose works were censored by the Vatican; the progressive evolutionism of Jacques Maritain (1882-1973); and the social personalism of Emmanuel Mounier (1905-1950).

The 1970s ushered a vigorous current of reformist thought that unmasked the true cause of underdevelopment, poverty, social alienation, and widespread popular discontent. The Third World was being immolated so that the First World could continue to enjoy the fruits of its overabundance. More and more theologians became pastors, militant agents of inspiration for the grassroots life of the church. They took part in discussions about the origin, nature, and limits of human knowledge in learned synods and congresses then returned to their parishes among the people where they immersed themselves in matters of ministry, trade unionism, and community organization. Thus, Liberation Theology spread and codified Christian faith as it applies to the needs of the poor. As these developments took place, misgivings followed by open hostility began to animate those who feared that faith was being over-politicized and others who mistook the redemptive nature of Liberation Theology for Bolshevism.

Predictably, in a region bled dry by war, devoured by corruption and economic decay, and enfeebled by harsh austerity measures to which the ruling elite is immune, Pope John Paul II's choice came as a shock and resonated like thunder throughout Latin America where dozens of activist priests were being fired and replaced by pliant champions of Catholic doctrinal extremism. According to the Rev. Joseph Mulligan, an American Jesuit I interviewed in Nicaragua, these clerics "tow the line very carefully on issues of doctrine. They are 'yes-men' doing Rome's bidding." As a result, Mulligan said, the Church "is suffering a pulling back from the strong commitment to social justice that marked the past five decades."

Now retired, Spanish-born Archbishop Saenz is a former Vatican liaison to the Salvadorian armed forces and a member of Opus Dei, the ultra-right-wing organization dedicated to promoting and enforcing Catholic dogma. His critics have accused him of cozying up to the ruling party, the plutocracy, and the military. Their claims are not without merit: Saenz accepted over one million dollars from the Salvadoran government and the country's richest families to resume erection of a cathedral left unfinished when Archbishop Romero proclaimed that it was "time to build the Church, not churches. Much to the dismay of

the Vatican, Romero had also long insisted
that it is blasphemy to indulge men's souls
while ignoring their earthly needs.

In a plea for "compassion," and in the
name of "national reconciliation," Saenz had
asked the government to pardon two former
national guardsmen convicted of raping and
killing three American nuns, Ita Ford, Maura
Clark, and Dorothy Kazel, and of a social
worker, Jean Donovan in 1980. The two soldiers served nineteen years of their 30-year
sentences. "Let us have mercy and pity for
them. They have demonstrated their repent-
ance," Saenz remarked without a trace of pity
or mercy for the victims and without ac-
knowledging that they had confessed to killing the women on the orders of superiors who
were never prosecuted. The victims' families,
who filed a suit against El Salvador's former
defense minister and the former director general of the National Guard, accusing them of
covering up the killings, believe the women
were murdered because officials suspected
they sympathized with leftist guerrillas.

Short on resources and influence but long
on memory, the people of Central America
were also mindful that former Salvadoran
President Armando Calderón Sol was a mem-

ber of the same political party that engineered Archbishop Romero's assassination and masterminded — under the command of death-squad leader, CIA stooge and U.S. Army School of the Americas alumnus, Roberto D'Aubuisson — the 1981 massacre of 900 men, women, and children in the village of El Mozote. Nor will they ever forget that the Pope paid a courtesy call on Calderón, that he cavorted with barrel-chested generals bristling with medals, and that he granted audiences to high-society women sporting low-cut dresses and dripping with diamonds — instead of kneeling at the grave of six Jesuits slain in 1989 by a Salvadoran Army death squad.

It was during an earlier visit to Central America that Pope John Paul II first clashed with Liberation Theology supporters. In Managua, Nicaragua, he publicly humiliated the Rev. Ernesto Cardenal, a noted writer, philosopher, and social activist who would later be suspended from the priesthood. The Pontiff would "retire" scores of vocal Latin American liberal clerics. The headstrong or the unrepentant, among them Rev. Bertrand Aristide of Haiti and Rev. Fernando Cardenal (Ernesto's brother), would also be unceremoniously defrocked.

♦

Hastened by papal nepotism strongly biased in favor of die-hard bishops, this dilution in the ranks of progressive clergy has gained new impetus in Latin America. Tragically, in the most Catholic domain on earth, Jesus' message of compassion and peace has been subverted by martial attitudes that view the flock as the very enemies of the state. Astute and opportunistic, the Church continues to tap into the reactionary power base to maintain both doctrinal monopoly and political custody over the masses. There is a precedent — and a disquieting parallel. Nine hundred years ago, bloodhounds of orthodoxy sniffed out heretics and the carnage began. People who held unacceptable views were thrown into dungeons. There, they were tortured with inventive cruelty then killed. They were accused of harboring heterodox opinions. They were forced to confess that they worshipped the devil (translation: they were freethinkers); that they engaged in heretical pursuits (they hungered for knowledge); and that they conspired against the established order (they spoke out against corruption and intellectual turpitude).

The Church's obscene quest for supremacy, inspired and abetted by successive papal dynasties, was prelude to six "Crusades" during which hundreds of thousands of "infidels" — Muslims and Jews — were slaughtered in the name of "God." The same religious fervor fanned nearly four centuries of inquisitorial frenzy that devoured Europe and sent another half a million innocent people to the stake while their possessions, confiscated as "evidence," fattened the Vatican's building coffers.

♦

Not unlike Karl Marx, who scorned the proletariat, the Church has never fully expiated its contempt for the masses, atoned for its feigned homophobia, apologized for its blazing misogyny. It furiously rejects the notion that people can govern their conscience without its despotic guidance or control. Worse, it denies them the right to manage their political destinies by consigning their existence to the same Pharisaic elite that Jesus rebuked.

Few of Christianity's rulers, however outwardly pious, have lived up to the teachings of Jesus, the Jewish radical who preached compassion, pacifism, and egalitarianism. Faced with a choice between Jesus' ethic and political expediency, Pope John Paul and his successor, the expediently retired Benedict XVI, opted for the latter. They came to Latin America and told the poor that poverty is good. They then urged the rich to reject materialism — they might as well have sweet-talked hyenas into giving up a simmering carcass. In Mexico, donning silk and gilded vestments, Benedict — who had looked the other way when anecdotal reports of sexual misconduct by some of his foot soldiers soon revealed a global pattern of priestly promiscuity — called for a return to "traditional Christian values." A day later, in Cuba, he praised democracy then flew back to his sumptuous lodgings in the Vatican, the world's richest and most autarchic empire. In casting out the good shepherds of Christianity from the fold, both John Paul II and his successor also surrendered the flock to the carnivores.

No one should be surprised. The Vatican is an illegal and rogue state created in 1933 by a "Concordat" between the Nazis and the Church on condition that it endorse its patron's policies and objectives. The "Holy See" did not disappoint Hitler and his goons.

Its anti-democratic, anti-progressive strategies are best exemplified by its colossal retreat from reality and shameless disconnect from humankind.

HOMO HOMINIS LUPUS

U sed with discretion, the Internet is a fount of information. It can also be a cesspool of lies, gossip, partisan humbug, and barefaced hoopla crafted not to inform or enlighten but to skew reality—or bury it—in the pursuit of mischief or zealotry. Sometimes, these half-truths and fabrications are subtle and alluring. Unrelated and irrelevant details are elegantly joined at the hip to erect impressive but improbable monuments of absurdity. More often, the ideas purveyors of "revealed knowledge" put forward, the "facts" they present, and the fears they inspire are so outlandish that they end up in the vast and ghostly cauldron of conspiracy theories where they simmer, swell, and stink.

Who can forget Australian journalist Jane Burgermeister's claim in 2009 that the bird flu vaccine was deliberately tainted to trigger a deadly pandemic? About seven million people died of cancer that year; half a million suffered fatal heart attacks; fewer than five thousand died of the flu. In fact fewer than ten deaths are linked to vaccine-related allergic reactions.

Another rumor, no less ominous but infinitely more titillating, was the alleged emergence of a New World Order—a sinister bureaucratic, collectivist government headed by a powerful and secretive assortment of globalists conniving to rule the planet and supplant legitimate sovereign nation-states. Political and financial tremors, social upheavals, and wars were blamed on a pulp fiction-style cabal engineered by various front organizations to achieve world domination. Before the early 1990s, New World Order conspiracism was limited to two U.S. subcultures, rabidly anti-government right-wing "patriots," and fundamentalist Christians obsessed with the rise of the Antichrist. A right-wing sub-conspiracy theory about a New World Order claims that it has infected popular culture, thereby inaugurating an unrivaled period in which people are actively preparing for an apocalyptic millenarian end-time scenario.

Hype merchants warn this phenomenon may cause the far right and the far left to "join forces" and launch an insurrectionary national-anarchist movement that will destroy the established system of governance. These comic-book scenarios are generally concocted by blogosphere jokesters and for-hire professional agitators, and peddled by chronic malcontents so bored with their lives that they need to spice them up by granting themselves a foretaste of a fictitious doomsday they conveniently leave to others to avert.

It is always tempting to attribute the dirty deeds men do to "conspiracies." The truth may be more prosaic—a rerun of human nature in the context of unfolding history: Supersized egos. Unfettered ambition. Greed. Larceny. Conquest. Domination. Subjugation. Persecution. Stealing from the poor to enrich the hyper-rich. Ruthless soldiers crowning themselves king. Clever accountants becoming bankers. Wealthy lawyers entering politics. Flag-waving cadets aspiring to field commands. Diminutive corporals dreaming of empire. What is being played before us is not some dastardly, covert scheme by a "chosen few" to rule the world. They rule it already. They always did; they always will. Feudal lords controlled their vassals' lives; slave owners, their chattels. In theocratic states, "spiritual leaders" and the "morality brigades" redefine and limit men's destinies. In some industrialized nations, it's the capitalists at home, the death squads in other people's backyards. In totalitarian countries, it's the secret police and the gulags. That's adaptive evolution. Smart, strong-willed, ambitious, imaginative, self-reliant, and ruthless men always claw their way to the top. Others fall to the wayside.

Life itself is "conspiratorial" parasitic biogenic process. Some of it takes place at the atomic level: White cells attack red cells, malignant tumors devour healthy tissue. A permanent change in the DNA sequence causes irreversible mutations. At the macro-politico-socio-economic level, elites exploit the masses; the profit-motive eclipses morality. It's in the nature of man to scheme, conspire, lie, cheat and, if need be, kill to achieve his aims. Large dinosaurs ate small dinosaurs. Big fish eat little fish. Powerful men make minced meat of lesser men. Sometimes, as is the case with certain inconvenient truths, imperiled special interests strike back with conspiracy theories of their own. They will assert that verifiable, observable phenomena such as global warming is being manipulated to strengthen the argument for technology-caused climate changes. What they fear, in fact, is that mounting evidence of man's carbon imprint on nature's delicate balance will weaken states' "rights" and wreak havoc with Libertarian agendas — including the self-granted entitlement to foul the atmosphere with noxious emissions, to dump toxic wastes into oceans, rivers and lakes, and to retard or suppress the advent of environment-friendly legislation.

Homo hominis lupus. Man is a wolf to man.[2]

---

[2] With apologies to the wolf, a far nobler animal than man.

GENOCIDE BY ANY OTHER NAME
SMELLS JUST AS BAD

Genocide is the "premeditated expulsion and mass murder of a people because of its indelible identity — race, ethnicity, religion, culture, and language." I choose this definition over others for its clarity and latitude.

The Armenian Genocide, also known as the Great Calamity, refers to the forcible deportation and slaughter of some one-and-a-half million Armenians during the Young Turks regime (1915-1917) in the Islamic Turkish-ruled Ottoman Empire. Turkey has steadfastly rejected the characterization of these events as "genocide" on semantic grounds and to serve its self-justifying political, religious, and revisionist agendas. The events are widely acknowledged as one of the first modern ethnic cleansings and many sources point to the sheer scale of the death toll as evidence of a sustained and methodical plan to thin out or eliminate an entire people. Known to have inspired Hitler, it is the second most studied case of genocide after the Jewish Holocaust, or Shoah. Responding to Turkish denials, twenty-two countries and forty U.S. states have adopted formal resolutions recognizing the Armenian genocide as a bona fide historical fact.

In 1914, an estimated two million Armenians lived in the Ottoman Empire. While many lived in Eastern Anatolia, many others inhabited the western part of Turkey, notably in and around Constantinople (Istanbul). It was nearly eighteen years earlier, though, that the first massacres in Anatolia began.

In 1896, The New York Times quoted a Turkish embassy gazette which, in a crass attempt at deflecting blame, alleged that "… it wasn't the Ottoman Court that caused the massacres in Anatolia but Christian propaganda in Asia Minor where the cry, 'Down with Islam,' triggered the war of the crescent against the cross." By the end of the 19th century, after a series of mass executions in 1894 and 1895, The New York Times noted an "apparent policy of extermination directed against Christians in Asia Minor."

In 1909, as the nascent Young Turk government splintered, thirty thousand Armenians perished during the Adana Massacre. Some thirteen hundred Assyrians and a number of Greeks were also slaughtered. In 1914, the Ottoman Empire entered WWI on the side of Germany, Austro-Hungary, and Bulgaria. Turkey launched an unsuccessful military campaign against Russia and accused the Armenians in the region of siding with the Russians. By 1914, Ottoman authorities had already begun a propaganda drive to portray Armenians living in Turkey as a threat to the country's security. A year later Turkey rounded up, imprisoned, and later executed two hundred and fifty intellectuals. The cabinet passed the Law of Expropriation and Confiscation, legalizing the deportation of Armenians and ruling that all property, including land, livestock, and homes belonging to Armenians, was to be seized.

The slaughter that ensued outraged the western world. While Turkey's wartime allies did not protest, German and Austrian documents quote the witnesses' horror at the killings and mass starvation of Armenians. Armenians were force-marched into the Syrian desert. Compelling evidence suggests that the Turks did not provide for their sustenance, neither during the exile, nor when they arrived. Deprived of their belongings, food, and water, thousands died.

In August 1915, The New York Times reported that "the roads and the Euphrates [river] are strewn with corpses, and those who survive are doomed to certain death. It is a plan to exterminate the whole Armenian people." Theodore Roosevelt characterized the carnage as "the greatest crime of the war." Calling it a holocaust, Winston Churchill wrote, "There is no reason to doubt that this crime was planned and executed for political reasons. The opportunity presented itself for clearing Turkish soil of a Christian race opposed to all Turkish ambitions."

Despite overwhelming evidence, denial by successive Turkish regimes continued from 1915 to the present. Out of political expediency—or moral turpitude—other governments, including those of the U.S. and, inexplicably Israel, aided and abetted Turkey in rewriting history.

Fast forward. In 2007 then Secretary of State Condoleezza Rice and Defense Secretary Robert Gates signed an open letter to Congress, warning that formal recognition of the Armenian Genocide "could harm American troops in the field [Iraq, Afghanistan] by antagonizing Turkey." Later that year, prior to a vote by the House that officially condemned the Great Calamity as genocide, Rice insisted the measure be defeated to "protect American regional interests and maintain basing rights in Turkey [where about five thousand U.S. military personnel are deployed] for American efforts in Iraq."

♦

While one may question the timeliness or pro forma nature of the House measure one could also ask what harm is there in a symbolic gesture that memorializes a real event that has left deep scars on the Armenian people. Remembering an incident that has been nearly universally acknowledged—and conveniently swept under the rug of history—would do the soul immense good. By rejecting the resolution, the Bush administration demonstrated that it was less interested in morality than its strategic self-interest. Claims by Senator Mitch McConnel, then minority leader, that an event more than a century old does not merit revisiting is absurd and contemptible.[3] Every bestial act that man has committed against humanity, from the Crusades and the Inquisition to the rape of Native America to Hiroshima and Nagasaki, to all the sectarian wars that now rage around the world, must be hammered in the consciousness of every school child, everywhere, until the end of time.

---

[3] The hard-right obstructionist senior senator from Kentucky would later use his political muscle to advance the erosion of democracy in the U.S.

SWEET LAND OF LIBERTY

A new kind of inquisition has been sweeping America. Less grisly but no less ominous than the demented and bloody witchhunts that convulsed Europe for three centuries, this latter-day pursuit of heretics has put on a fresh visage.

The government now spies on electronic communications, invades online privacy, regulates media coverage of the news, and crushes dissent. In the wake of the 9/11 attacks, White House Secretary Ari Fleischer's admonition that Americans "ought to watch out what they say" [later deleted from official transcripts] spoke volumes about the lightning speed with which constitutionally protected dissent suddenly becomes disloyalty and treachery.

In California, Democratic Rep. Barbara Lee, who had voted against congressional authorization for retaliatory military action in Iraq, was the subject of death threat and was forced to retain the services of a security detail. Rep. Jim McDermott, D.-WA; a vocal critic of U.S. foreign policy in Latin America — I had interviewed him in Guatemala in 1994 — would repeatedly come under fire for advocating restraint and expressing strong reservations about a military response.

Academics, students, labor leaders, progressive members of the clergy, and journalists would also come under attack for questioning the need and wisdom of war. TV talk show host Bill Maher and philosopher/filmmaker Susan Sontag were excoriated for their humanist views. The Dixie Chicks, probably the most "down home" American country music group, were reviled and boycotted by enraged "patriots."

The Patriot Act, a sinister piece of legislation enacted 45 days after the attacks on the World Trade Center and the Pentagon, and rammed through with virtually no debate, gave the president broad powers while shielding the government from scrutiny and oversight. It rescinded checks and balances on law enforcement and threatened the very rights and freedoms that Americans had been struggling to protect.

The FBI, without warrant or probable cause, snooped on credit ratings, confidential medical records, library files, and student transcripts. The Act also put the CIA back in the business of spying on Americans. Once gleaned, the information could be shared without a court order.

In a reaffirmation that "eminent domain" is tantamount to sanctioned thievery, came news that a divided Supreme Court had ruled that local governments, in a reverse Robin Hood fashion — take from the poor, give to the rich — may seize people's homes and businesses against their will for private development. Assailed by dissenting Supreme Court Justice Sandra Day O'Connor as "handing disproportionate influence and power" to the well-heeled, the 5-4 ruling in the case of Kelo v. New London was a slap in the face of Connecticut residents whose homes were slated for demolition to make room for an office complex. They had argued that cities have no right to seize their lands except for public projects such as roads, schools or bridges, or to revitalize blighted areas. As a result, cities seeking to generate tax revenues can now bulldoze residences to make room for shopping malls and hotels.

O'Connor, who had often been a key swing vote, issued a stinging dissent, arguing that cities should not have unlimited authority to uproot families, even in exchange for compensation, simply to accommodate wealthy developers.

"Any property may now be taken for the benefit of another private party, but the fallout from this decision will not be random," she wrote prophetically. "The beneficiaries are likely to be those citizens with disproportionate influence and power in the political process, including large corporations and developers."

The report further asserts that operating largely out of public view—in tax court, through obscure legislative loopholes, and in private negotiations with the Internal Revenue Service—the rich use their power to steadily whittle away at the government's ability to tax them. The result has been the creation of a se-

cretive and elitist tax system catering to a se-
lect few Americans.

With economic inequality at its highest
level in nearly a century and public debate rising over whether the government should react
by imposing higher taxes on the wealthy, an
article published last December in the New
York Times, alleges that plutocrats quietly
shape tax policy in their favor and that the
wealthiest Americans have financed an arcane
and shockingly effective apparatus for shelter-
ing their fortunes from scrutiny.

◆

And then, in a display of childish petulance
and chauvinism, the House approved a consti-
tutional amendment that would give Congress
the power to ban desecration of the American
flag. The measure was designed to overturn a
1989 decision by the Supreme Court which
ruled 5-4 that flag-burning is a protected free-
speech right. The Senate was expected to consider the measure after the July 4 holiday ...
when America is traditionally and perfunctorily festooned with Old Glory.

How the amendment to punish "desecration" — whether by flogging, drawing-and-

quartering, burning at the stake, a year in jail or twelve months of public service in a flag factory — was not clear. Supporters argued that the measure reflected the patriotism that deepened after the September 11 terrorist attack. They accused detractors of being out of touch with America's sentiments. Rep. Jerrold Nadler, D-NY, responded, saying that "If the flag needs protection at all, it needs to be protected from members of Congress who value the symbol more than the freedoms that the flag represents."

Desecrating a flag, any flag, is an act of colossal immaturity and idiocy that justifiably merits contempt; but it is not a crime. Making it so will only serve to underscore and bolster the vindictive fury and aberrant jingoism that all too often convulses America. It will also trivialize every ideal that the flag represents and pledges to protect.

Liberties relinquished are difficult, sometimes impossible, to reclaim. Vulnerable in times of crisis, they are easy prey when "national security" (translation — the bulimic appetite of the capitalist engine) is invoked.

Where will it end?

"GOD'S WARRIORS" OR THE DEVILS?

I come from a family that never mentioned "God" — except as an interjection. I was not given a religious education (nor deprived of one) but the notion of an invisible, omnipotent creator/arbiter/destroyer seemed to me ludicrous even as a child.

By the time I was old enough to fathom the enormity of my parents' suffering, especially during and after WWII, they had turned agnostic — my father's early rabbinical studies and my mother's pseudo-assimilation into a Gentile mainstream notwithstanding. Struck with pancreatic cancer, my mother died after months of martyrdom, convinced that religion is a travesty. Heartbroken, my father, a physician whose parents and two brothers perished in one of Hitler's extermination camps, cried out against the fragility of life and the failings of medicine.

He and I had long chats about religion. We agreed that the underpinnings of religion—mysticism, the supernatural, blind faith in an unknowable entity, the rituals and strident taboos—were all contrived to enslave man, not liberate him. We acknowledged the nobility of the "Golden Rule," present in Judaism, Christianity, Islam, yet noted man's inclination to ignore it, even violate it, in the name of Yahweh, Theos, and Allah. We pored over Hillel the Elder, the first century BCE rabbi who wrote, "What is hateful to you, do not do to your neighbor." We read Luke 6:31: "Treat others as you want them to treat you." We turned to the Qur'an: "None of you is a believer until he wishes for his brother that which he wishes for himself." But "others," "neighbors," and "brother," we realized, have a parochial meaning that signifies "those of our own kind—*us*, not *them*.

This paradox was astutely dissected by CNN journalist Christiane Amanpour. Aired in 2007, the three-part, award-winning documentary "God's Warriors: The Clash Between Piety and Politics," offered a disturbing rendering of religion's susceptibility to intolerance in the service of deity and of its assault on secular society. It also examined the rise of religious fundamentalism—Jewish, Christian, and Muslim—as a political force in the world.

Only religious delirium could inspire a Muslim father to plot the "honor killing" of his own daughter, or to bomb a disco filled with Jewish youths. Only numinous rapture could lead a self-styled Christian to murder doctors performing legal abortions. Only Jewish zealots could torch cars on the Sabbath (in clear violation of biblical injunctions), assault Jews marching at a Gay Pride Parade, and murder Muslims praying peacefully in their mosque.

The record shows that the prime targets of religious hatred are "heretics," a one-size-fits-all label that singles out those who hold different beliefs than one's own, or who grant themselves the right to hold none. Within that conflict rests an unresolved tension between the command to love one's enemies and the equally strong directive to reject any alien or divergent dogma. Neither Jew, nor Christian or

Muslim knows which of the two decrees to obey at any given time. By attacking "heretics" as tools of Satan, religious fanatics seize the rhetorical high ground and shift the focus from loving one's enemies to the escapist option of eradicating an imaginary but prescriptive source of evil.

This was the dominant rationale for nine Crusades, the "Holy" Inquisition, the Thirty Years' War, the centuries-old strife in Northern Ireland, the Armenian and Jewish Holocausts, the Hutu-Tutsi reciprocal slaughter in Rwanda, the Hindu-Muslim-Sikh conflict in India and Kashmir, the bloodbath in Sudan, and the unending Shiite-Sunni discord.

Nor has hatred of "heretics" spared America now that proliferating dynasties of charlatan preachers and megachurches have hijacked the nation's psyche while rifling through its pockets. Most alarming is the religious fundamentalists' stated mission to infiltrate and exploit the coercive power of government. The U.S. has a long implied tradition of separating church and state, but it has done nothing to protect against the intrusion of religion into the body politic. We have seen religion ever more deeply woven into the fabric of governance. The Constitution guarantees the non-involvement of government in religion, but it has failed to hinder religion from muscling in on the affairs of state. In the long run, such politically motivated laissez-faire could transform America into a citadel of intolerance and an incubator for hatred. It could also invite theocratic control.

A LAMP THAT SHEDS NO LIGHT

O   *h time! Suspend your flight. Reality be gone. Step right up to the dreamscape, the magic lamp is on.* It's an ancient incantation but the spell works like a charm. Take the animated movie, Aladdin, which I found myself watching the other day on TV. Based loosely on the Arabian Nights, a collection of Middle Eastern folk tales dating as far back as the 12th century, the Oscar-winning Disney feature film traces the rags-to-riches of an impoverished young ne'er-do-well in a mythical exotic realm. The trailer touts the film as "family-friendly and goofy."

Aided by hindsight, informed by experience, I had quickly surmised when I first saw it that no sooner out of the ink bottle, the film would generate millions of dollars from video rights, T-shirts, toys, mugs, coloring books, and other marketing ploys.[4] In an age of impoverished imagination and waning originality, there is nothing like a great old legend reworked to conceal a dearth of ideas. Such artifice would be easily shrugged off were it not for the fact that, in reinventing Aladdin, the street child, Disney missed a golden opportunity to speak out on life in the streets, to explore with realism and empathy the consequences of an unenviable fate shared today by one hundred and fifty million children around the globe. It settled instead on a cartoon version of a fairy tale, complete with heroes who invariably triumph over cruel but strangely lovable villains.

---

[4] Released on November 25, 1992 to critical and commercial success, Aladdin became that year's blockbuster film, with earnings of over $500 million in worldwide box office revenues. Upon release, it became the first animated feature to reach the half–billion-dollar mark, and was briefly the highest-grossing animated film of all time. Meanwhile the number of homeless minors continues to grow globally.

When fact clashes with set perceptions or deep-rooted sensibilities, the cinema industry will not hesitate to bury the truth. The celluloid Aladdin, later reprised on Broadway by a human thespian, and since warmed over yet again on film, is the street child we can all safely love. Half imp, half angel, resourceful, generous, articulate, spirited and awfully cute, he is the freshly scrubbed, born-again two-dimensional idealization of childhood denied and innocence undone, the colorized, sanitized avatar of real young castaways who live in fear and often die a brutal death. If Aladdin's re-creators cannot be accused of deliberate deception, they are guilty of inspiring sham sympathy and granting hypocrisy a public forum. Offered an escape from reality, the child in us all too easily surrenders to fantasy. Willing participants, we are lulled back to that wondrous, carefree time when the world was new and safe, when life was forever.

Myth obviates memory. It anesthetizes reason. Mercifully, it silences the truth. Fiction also trivializes fact. There is no romance in the lives of street children, only pain and hopelessness, hunger and terror, abuse, disease, and premature demise. Real street children do not sport beguiling smiles. They misbehave. They often stink. All could use a bath. But under the grime, the air of defiance or the crushing indifference their feverish eyes convey, there is a child, scared, at risk, far too young to be tasting life's bitter medicine, yet incurably old before his time.

In the ghostly twilight world of street children, there are no magic lamps, no benevolent turbaned genies, no flying carpets, no amulets. No healing potions, only evil spirits lurking, stalking easy prey. Unlike Aladdin, street children do not achieve fame and fortune and no fairy prince or princess will marry them in the end. Most never leave the streets. Many don't reach adulthood. Sickness, hunger, drugs, and bullets often cut their lives short.

As I watched, my mind turned to a particularly bloody year in Guatemala when some fifty homeless children were "eliminated" in an unrelenting government-sponsored, police-led campaign of extermination. A year later, uniformed men in a jeep with tinted windows kidnapped eight street children from a downtown neighborhood. The bodies of three of the boys all bore the telltale signs of vigilante justice. Their ears had been cut off, their eyes gouged. And in a time-honored warning against snitching, their tongues had been carved out. The other boys were never found. Their tormentors, as are those of hundreds of other homeless children who shared a similar fate, are still at large. Similar "purges" took place in Honduras at the hands of police and private security guards. Hopefully, they all died quickly. But that's not always the way things happen in Central America, not for the street kids, the defenseless, the voiceless, the pariahs, the nonconformists, the meddlesome journalists, and the dissidents. For them is reserved a special kind of inhumanity that draws its power from the top echelons of government and an impunity fed by the craven apathy of the masses.

Aladdin is a charming cartoon and a cinematographic tour de force. Its fundamental weakness is that it teaches no real lesson. Worse, is allows a compliant public easily charmed by the antics of two-dimensional characters to turn a blind eye to the flesh-and-blood orphans and rejects of a human family in disarray. In so doing, Aladdin fails his own kind. Where important values are at stake, entertainment is simply not enough.

A lamp must focus on the truth or it sheds no light at all.

CHEWING THE FAT

Fat and laughing all the way to the bank the airline industry is not to be pitied but the ongoing flap over how to deal with over-weight passengers has turned into a public relations nightmare and an impasse. Airlines are in a squeeze and they appear to be caving in to political correctness by caving in to a strident few while ignoring the inalienable comfort of the many. Heavy suitcases aren't the only things weighing down airplanes and forcing them to burn more fuel. A government study suggests that airlines are now mulling over the weight of their human cargo.

Yes, they are big, masses of lumbering, redundant fat that alters their gait, stresses their bones, fatigues their heart, and shortens their lives. They are the severely overweight and they will soon surpass those suffering from malnutrition. Diet-related health problems in America are not quite as exotic as starvation in Bangladesh or Burundi. American's don't like to forage in their own backyards. They'd rather commiserate, or pretend to, with nameless, faceless people in distant lands. It eases their conscience — while they eat the rest of the world under the table. Voyeurism may be America's premier pastime but self-scrutiny is not a deeply-rooted tradition. It interferes with our overblown self-view which everyone knows is what endows us our swaggering nature. Such conceit, alas, also blinds us to the dangers of overindulgence.

Obesity in America has set off predictable alarms. It's an epidemic, with catastrophic consequences. Obese individuals have a higher-than-normal incidence of hypertension, Type 2 diabetes, high lipid concentrations, cardiovascular and bladder disease, osteoarthritis, strokes, respiratory disease, and cancer.

According to a report by the Worldwatch Institute, a record two billion people are habitually underfed. In contrast, a like number are gorging themselves, mostly on junk, nutrient-deficient food. A third category that overlaps the other two is poetically described as the "hidden hungry," those who may appear to be well nourished but are weakened by an absence of essential vitamins and minerals in their diet. The report blames the soaring number of eating disorders in America on "a way of life where physical activity is so rare and so trivial that caloric intake greatly exceeds caloric outlay. This surplus is transformed into unsightly, health-endangering fat." There is a tragic absurdity to this trend. Whereas millions of children die of malnutrition or starvation around the world every year, about half a million Americans spend $10 billion on liposuction procedures; another 200,000 undergo gastric bypass surgery. Meanwhile—from the sublime to the ridiculous—seats on the Puget Sound ferry had to be widened from eighteen to twenty inches. A number of ambulances in Colorado had to be outfitted with hydraulic winches capable of lifting 1,000-pound humans. Supersized caskets are now available— 38 inches wide instead of 24!

Nationwide, a record number of "handicapped" decals and license plates have been issued to motorists whose handicap is widely regarded as self-inflicted.[5] The Worldwatch Institute report also asserts that the two extremes of hunger and obesity are increasing in all societies, rich and poor. The ratio of overweight individuals in Brazil and Colombia skyrocketed to 31 percent and 43 percent respectively.

"Obesity has always been a sign of prosperity in Latin America," a Honduran journalist once told me. "A big beer belly, a barrel chest, and a double chin telegraph success. Cutting an imposing figure in business and social circles is worth its weight in gold."[6] By contrast, India, where obesity is also common in pockets of affluence, has the world's largest number of underweight, malnourished minors. According to David Barker, an epidemiologist at Southampton University, "60 per-

---

[5] My late father, a skilled and dedicated physician who had no patience for malingerers and hypochondriacs, once remarked that many people who blame their weight and girth on a "glandular condition" probably consider their mouth a gland.

[6] Driving a Jaguar, Porsche or BMW in Honduras, a country boasting crater-sized potholes and wallowing in abject poverty, is another ego-boosting device among the ten filthy rich dynastic families that misgovern it.

cent of all infants in India would be in intensive care had they been born in California."

Interdependent, poverty and unfettered fertility, rather than food shortages, are the underlying causes of hunger in some parts of the world. About 80 percent of all undernourished children live in countries enjoying food surpluses that are generally exported. "In an age of unprecedented global prosperity, it is ironic and shameful for malnutrition to exist on such a massive scale," the Worldwatch Institute's report concludes. On the other hand, gluttony, a relative of the insatiable craving we have for big things, also sharpens our lust for large, calorie-packed, sugar-laden, salt-packed, fat-producing meals.

As these excesses and dichotomies unfold, Merrill Lynch, the investment bank, is offering psychiatric counseling to the children of America's fastest growing minority—the multimillionaires—to help ward off "affluenza," a chronic and often fatal malady that turns rich kids into dissolute, weak-willed, profligate little monsters.

Yes, it's a mad, mad world of self-indulgence and insufficiency, extravagance and wrenching want. Some spend their last hard-earned centavo to feed their children;

others devour food as if there was no tomorrow. Others yet hire shrinks to speak to their children about the value of money and the management of wealth. Some must trim the fat, others live on it. Go figure.

VOYAGE OF THE DAMNED

Every year, in February, I turn to a now forgotten event, the first of two incomprehen-
sible acts of premeditated mass murder. Both
would be eclipsed by the convulsions of a
world at war then trivialized by the passage of
time.

On December 12, 1941, fleeing the pogroms in Nazi-occupied Romania, 778 Romanian and Russian Jews embarked in the Black
Sea port of Constanza on a small vessel of du-
bious sea-worthiness, bound for then British-
controlled Palestine. Under the command of a
Bulgarian captain and flying the Panamanian

flag, the ship was known as the MV Struma.

The crossing had been approved by Romania's fascist dictator {later convicted war criminal] Ion Antonescu. All too eager to rid his country of the *jidans*, as Jews are still pejoratively called in Romania, Antonescu understood the consequences of his benevolence. Passengers, who had each paid $1,000 ($20,000 in today's currency) to make the voyage, had been kept away from the wharf where the Struma was docked. When they boarded they were shocked to discover a greasy, dilapidated, malodourous rust bucket. Sleeping quarters were primitive, filthy, and cramped. There were only two lifeboats. Worse, the engine did not work. It had been salvaged from a wreck dredged from the bottom of the Danube River and hastily fitted in the Struma's bowels.

Adrift for three days, the ship was towed to Istanbul where it remained at anchor while "secret negotiations" were being held over the fate of its human freight. With diminishing food and water reserves, lacking proper sanitation facilities, conditions on the intolerably crowded Struma worsened.

In the wake of violent unrest within Palestine, which had collaborated with the Third

Reich, the British government was determined to halt Jewish immigration and urged the Turkish authorities to prevent the Struma from reaching its intended destination. The Turks complied by preventing engine repairs and forbidding passengers from disembarking or staying in Turkey.

On the evening of February 23, 1932, after 70 days at sea, Turkish police seized control of the disabled ship and towed it through the Bosporus into open waters where it continued to drift. At dawn, a single torpedo launched from a Russian submarine tore into the Struma's hull, splitting it in half. A jubilant cable from the "junior officers, unit commander, and non-commissioned officers" reported that the "SC-213 submarine encountered an unprotected enemy vessel — the SS Struma. Our crew showed courage and the ship was successfully disabled from a distance of 1,118 meters [3,600 ft.] and sunk." That day 103 children, 269 women, and 406 men died, among them two members of my family. Turkish authorities did not conduct rescue operations for more than twenty four hours.[7]

---

[7] The lone survivor, David Stoliar, died on May 1, 2014 at the age of 91 in Bend, Oregon.

Before dawn, on August 5, 1944, sailing under the Turkish and Red Cross flags, the MV Mefkura, a wooden-hulled schooner chartered to carry Romanian refugees to Istanbul, was suddenly illuminated by flares from an unknown vessel. The Mefkura failed to respond and sailed on. It was then fired on and began to sink. Only five of the 350 passengers survived. Like the MV Struma, the Mefkura, it was later learned, had been torpedoed by a Soviet submarine.

◆

In-your-face, prime-time images of man's inhumanity to man don't lie. Our world, history and the evening news remind us, is a sewer in which we wade knee-deep in the blood of martyrs. Gathered around the dinner table, we watch them die or fade away like ghosts. "Past is prelude," we intone with snooty condescension. We owe it to our fragile, overtaxed psyches to forget an endless stream of atrocities: The methodical extermination of Native Americans, the Armenian and Jewish holocausts, Biafra, the inter-tribal Hutu-Tutsi carnage, the bloodbath in Chiapas, Mexico and the Guatemalan highlands, Bosnia, the 70-

year-long bloodletting that continues to envenom relations between Israelis and Palestin-
ians, Sudan, Iraq, Afghanistan, and the wan-
ton and ongoing assassination of Central
American street children by agents of the state
trained by the US.

Natural disasters shock us to our core and
remind us of our own mortality. The scenes
we replay in our minds are reinforced by a
steady diet of gruesome or heart-rending images compliments of our local TV networks.
Then fatigue sets in—emotional exhaustion—
and we tire of the spectacle that had kept us
spellbound and anguished for a brief moment.
Distance, racial differences, and cultural incongruities, all help intellectualize other peoples' agony. We endure it by perfunctorily
purging our souls after each act of infamy.
"You can't change human nature," we pontifi-
cate, as we partake of dessert. In a pinch, a
witless sitcom will help set our minds at ease.
We survive the truth by looking the other
way.

IN XIBALBA'S ENTRAILS

From the mists of time, deep in the primeval Guatemalan jungles, comes a document known as the Popol Vuh, a fragmentary chronicle of the allegories, beliefs, and traditions of the Maya. An epic poem of great lyric beauty and haunting melancholy, the Popol Vuh is also a record of the peregrinations of a people caught in life's eternal struggle for survival, identity, and cultural self-affirmation. The Maya feared death more than any of life's inescapable ordeals and only exceptional individuals, they claimed could find their way to the heavenly gates. The unworthy were hastily dispatched to Xibalba—the Maya hell, the "House of Gloom," the "World of Ghosts," the "Mansion of the Damned"—an abyss teeming with monsters where they endured ceaseless cold, hunger, and other agonies.

If the Maya took great pains to elude such unenviable fate (self-mutilation and orgiastic human sacrifices, they believed, could forestall the inevitable) they had no illusion that life "on the surface" was apt to be just as hideous as in Xibalba's entrails. Ego, greed, cruelty, deceit, vengeance prevailed, all acted out with an incontinence bordering on lunacy. Blood lettings, warfare, decapitations, amputations, in short senseless carnage, were as likely to envenom their mortal existence as the "lower regions" to which their souls would eventually be consigned.

Longing for salvation, their leaders engaged in an endless consecration of grandiose ideals. Awaiting the advent of dawn but not the passage of greater events, they yearned for a spiritual reawakening that would never be. They pandered to heartless idols and vengeful spirits, and offered sacrifices to atone inexpiable sins while the masses were fated to a life of submission and servitude in the shadow of despotic and degenerate elites. Busy erecting flamboyant pantheons, obsessed with their own place in posterity, the cruel demigods the people idolized were no kinder than the bloodthirsty fiends of Xibalba. They knew they were false of heart, egotistical self-promoters, agents of evil, and tormentors of men, and that their extravagance and folly would lead to civil strife, social exhaustion and disintegration and, in due course, apocalypse. Eventually, the debauchery, the drug-induced stupor and psychotic outbursts, the bombastic mystique of their masters' esoteric pursuits began to wear thin in the eyes of the overburdened, exhausted populace.

"Of what practical value to us, illiterate Maya," they pondered, "are such abstractions as systems of reckoning dates, stargazing, and arcane hieroglyphics when this knowledge is the exclusive domain of the ruling class?" Too long had the peons been forced into a state of servitude, too exacting was the endless labor involved in erecting temples and sacrificial altars, tending the fields of the princely castes, and paying exorbitant tributes to corrupt and insensitive monarchs. For centuries the multitudes had surrendered to the ruling aristocracy; the sting of despotism, the ignominy of persecution would soon trigger a collective heave of revulsion followed by open rebellion.

Along with a sharp increase in the dominance of the aristocracy and the opulence and ostentation their lifestyle required, the number of underlings and petty functionaries needed to cater to their slightest whims grew to colossal proportions, This imposed additional burdens for food and other goods needed to sustain the hierarchy. It is likely that these stresses triggered ever-widening divisions and fed mounting hostilities between the lower classes and their bejeweled, quetzal-feathered masters.

There is now evidence in the Late Classical era—the period preceding the "fall"—of an unimpeded population explosion and a dizzying acceleration in the number and size of urban centers. All these pressures—overpopulation, extravagant demands by the plutocracy for goods and services, widening rifts between social strata—had a profound and everlasting impact on Maya civilization that left it teetering breathlessly on the brink. Mortally wounded, nudged by an irresistible momentum, the once great, the magnificent Maya quivered and dipped it over the edge.

Mel Gibson's 2006 blockbuster, Apocalypto, which focuses on a few days in the dizzying tug-of-war between life and death in early 16th century Mesoamerica, hints at the sudden and staggering collapse of a once-glorious empire. Savage, hypnotic, this disquieting film also suggests that famine, brought on by overpopulation and over-cultivation, crippling epidemics and widespread discontent with remote and narcissistic leaders would lead to economic collapse, anarchy, and diaspora.

For the surviving Maya (some four million live in southeastern Mexico, Guatemala, and Honduras) only two paths of survival remain—servitude and forced assimilation or alternating states of neglect and repression by the foreign despots who now occupy their ancestral lands. Like their tribal brothers and sisters in the region, they remain suspended between two contrasting and incongruous continuums—ancient (intimate and comforting) and modern (alien and menacing). In Central America, where prodigality and want, esotericism and frightening reality coexist in shameful proximity, Xibalba is a familiar signpost on the well-traveled road to nowhere. Sadly, for indigenous communities in the Isthmus, there is no exit ramp. New dynasties of rich and powerful overlords seem hell-bent on replicating the history that began when bearded savages brandishing a sword in one hand and the cross in the other, first landed on the pristine beaches of the "New World."

Mel Gibson is a gifted actor and brilliant moviemaker. Will he have the moral courage to crown the cinematic masterpiece that Apocalypto is with a sequel that picks up when half-naked natives glance toward the sea, terrified and uncomprehending, as alien craft filled with hirsute, helmeted devils slowly slink ashore? Could future blockbusters regale us with an honest glimpse at the horrors of the Crusades, which preceded the rape of Americas, and the "Holy Inquisition" which followed?

FLIGHT FROM TRUTH

There are wacky and spine-chilling conspiracy theories that are successfully debunked, and there are plausible but disquieting assertions that are secretively squelched, often in the name of "national security."

On page 16, in its Sunday, October 18, 1998 editorial section, The New York Times ran a full-page ad urging government agencies in bold banner headlines to "END THE COVER-UP" and asserting that "Two Missiles Brought Down TWA Flight 800." The ad was sponsored by the Associated Retired Aviation Professionals, a distinguished group headed by

Admiral Thomas Moorer, Rear-Admiral Mark Hill, U.S. Air Force Brigadier General, Ben Partin, U.S. Navy Commandeer William Donaldson, and three veteran military and civilian aviators, including the flight engineer who had flown on the inbound leg of TWA 800's flight from Athens the day before the plane went down off the coast of Long Island on July 17, 1996, as it proceeded toward Paris, and killing 230 people on board. The ad further affirmed that the FBI had interviewed one hundred and fifteen "credible eyewitnesses" who claimed to have seen an object believed to be a missile streak upward toward the airliner and explode.

From the start, FBI investigators suspected the disaster was the result of foul play but refused to release eyewitness statements; and the National Transportation Safety Board refused to let a single eyewitness appear at the highly publicized final hearing on the cause(s) of the tragedy. So why the secrecy? And why did the major media sheepishly go along with this devious suppression of eyewitness testimony?

Some have speculated that on the eve of the Atlanta Olympic Games, such revelation would have dampened the spirit of the event and severely impacted commercial interests. Moreover, looming presidential elections and a diplomatic deadlock in the Middle East further dictated that early conclusions by federal sleuths be modulated to resemble nebulous speculations. With mounting evidence all but eliminating mechanical failure as the single cause of the crash, and no compelling incentive to divulge the facts, investigators may have opted to withhold their findings as long as possible or, if need be, to shelve the awful truth in the "national interest."

◆

GENESIS. The ill-fated TWA Boeing 747 was the one hundred and fifty-third aircraft to roll out of the production line in 1971. It had since crisscrossed the globe without serious incident. A tire blew up on takeoff in 1987. An oil leak forced and engine shutdown a year later. Both flights reached their destinations uneventfully. Its penultimate voyage was also problem-free. It landed in Athens on Wednesday, July 17 at 11:32 and took off for New York at 13:25. Data gleaned from black boxes revealed no anomalous conditions prior to the conflagration that felled it later that evening.

Crew chatter, mostly routine post-takeoff protocol, betrayed no anxiety, no sense of foreboding. Only a brief snapping sound was heard just before the fatal silence. It was the same old "ping" picked up by the flight data recorders of two commercial aircraft destroyed in mid-flight — Pan Am 103, blown up when a Toshiba portable radio crammed with pentrite exploded over Lockerbie, Scotland in 1988, killing 270 people; and a DC-10 operated by France's now defunct feeder airline, UTA, which disintegrated at 33,000 feet over the African desert in 1989, killing 171. The culprit: 300 grams of pentaerythritol tetranitrate hidden in the cargo hold.

According to Tom Thurman, the FBI specialist who had investigated the Pan Am 103 explosion, the TWA 800 airliner in all likelihood was also destroyed by an on-board incendiary substance — "a few hundred grams of pentrite, C4, or Semtex." Odorless, easy to handle, these "smart" explosives can be triggered by altimetric or 24-hour timing devices. Thurman suspected that an explosive charge placed on the right side of the forward cargo hold, probably a suitcase, tore the aircraft at the seam where the wings join the fuselage. While it took a scant four days to determine that UTA's DC-10 had been felled by a bomb, ten months passed before the luggage in which it was concealed was identified. The telltale evidence was less than an inch in size. It took Thurman two years to determine how the booby-trapped Toshiba radio was secreted on board Pan Am 103 — and by whom.

◆

SABOTAGE? How could an explosive device have been spirited on board TWA 800? Speculations were rife:

- A "kamikaze" passenger might have concealed it in carry-on luggage. This theory was quickly dismissed; the explosion did not occur in the passenger cabin.
- The bomb made its way into the cargo hold in Athens and the timing device set to trigger the explosion as the plane made its way to Paris, not New York. Farfetched.
- It was secreted on board in New York, where security has been characterized as recently as 2018 by French counter-terrorism agents at Charles de Gaulle

> (CDG) Airport in Paris as "notoriously lax—if not downright inept." They likened security at JFK Airport to Swiss cheese—'full of holes."

- Baggage handlers or cleaning crews could have conspired. French intelligence had apprehended three known Islamic extremists working at CDG.

All airplane sabotage cases were solved—from the 1970 explosion of a Swissair Convair in Zurich, to the Boeing 747 that disintegrated over Lockerbie. Extremist states, in these cases Iran and Libya, were implicated. Preliminary investigations into the TWA 800 disaster did not discount sabotage and pointed to the Middle East where the U.S. was regarded as *Public Enemy Number One* by Islamic radicals.

◆

THE USUAL SUSPECTS. A prime and tempting suspect was Ramzi Yousef. Trained in Pakistan, Yousef was the mastermind behind the plot to destroy U.S. airlines over the Pacific. The plot was foiled. Captured in Pakistan in 1995, he was extradited to the U.S. Tried and convicted of engineering the 1993 World

Trade Center bombing, he is now serving two consecutive life sentences. No evidence of complicity in the TWA 800 crash was ever found.

The U.S. had also been threatened by Jamaa Islamya, the group responsible for the World Trade Center bombing. Now serving a life sentence at the Springfield, Missouri federal penitentiary, its spiritual leader, Sheik Omar Abdul Rahman, the blind cleric who conspired to bomb the United Nations and flood tunnels connecting New York and New Jersey, had vowed to get even.

Another hot lead — a new and mysterious terrorist cell responsible for attacks in Saudi Arabia, the first in Riyadh in 1995, in which five Americans were killed, the second in Dhahran, in 1996, in which 19 were killed and hundreds wounded. Intelligence sources claimed the group was run from Afghanistan where Osama bin Laden had sought asylum. Bin Laden had many friends in Pakistan's intelligence community. He also supported Hamas, the radical Palestinian group that had a score to settle with the U.S. when it considered extraditing him to Israel where he faced a life sentence. These groups have one thing in common: All are ultra-secret and highly fluid organizations with worldwide networks that are difficult if not impossible to infiltrate. Pakistan and Saudi Arabia, Syria, Iran, Iraq, and Libya had all professed a common hatred of the U.S. and Israel, and worked in concert to rekindle Islamic fervor and a collective anti-Western agenda. Algerian, Sudanese and Afghan operatives had long been training in Iran.

Another suspect with known ties to America's arch-enemy, Iran, is Hezbollah, the homicidal phalanx responsible for multiple suicide bombings in Israel. Hezbollah never forgave the U.S. for its support of Israel following the Qana massacre in Lebanon in April 1996 in which one hundred six civilians were killed and one hundred sixteen were wounded by Israeli artillery. Four years earlier, striking without warning, Hezbollah units had pulverized the Israeli embassy in Buenos Aires, killing twenty nine civilians and injuring two hundred and forty-two.

It is no secret that Iran trains and subsidizes global terrorist networks. A senior diplomat stationed in Central America told this writer on condition of anonymity: "I believe Iran is behind the downing of TWA 800." He rejected mechanical failure as the cause of the crash.

"Catastrophic failure, often referred to as an 'act of God,' is an expedient first-cause explanation. It is also an obliging rationalization that suits the political needs of the moment. It will have to do for the time being." The diplomat did not dismiss the possibility that France, not the U.S., was the intended target of this latest act of barbarism.

♦

UP, UP, AND AWAY. Tempting as they were, speculations about the "usual suspects" remained just that—theories bereft of empirical evidence. Chasing after very tenuous leads would have been time-consuming and involving lengthy, subtle and complex diplomacy. Americans wanted categorical, unambiguous answers—now. So investigators reluctantly set their sights on a culprit less traumatizing than "catastrophic mechanical failure." Asking that his identity be withheld, a veteran American Airlines captain told this writer in Miami that the TWA airliner "would have had to be stressed beyond the designed limits of structural endurance to break up in three pieces without the benefit of some colossal intervening dynamic, namely a massive detonation. A structural weakness," he added, "would have been detected during routine maintenance and promptly repaired." The pilot declined to speculate on the cause(s) of the detonation but hinted that mechanical failure was psychologically the least disturbing of all possible interpretations.

What remains is the nagging possibility, scrupulously described by eyewitnesses, that a missile friendly or hostile, felled TWA's Paris-bound jumbo jet. Fearing panic, then Secretary of State Warren Christopher publicly dismissed the "theory" as "highly improbable." Widespread and mounting, suspicions were never allayed; they just took on a life of their own. The deliberate spurning by investigators of witnesses who swore to have seen a "flare" or "rocket" light up the night sky seconds before the aircraft exploded, split apart, and hurtled into the waters of Long Island's south shore, continues to fuel speculations.

A Continental Airlines pilot I interviewed in Houston in 1999 was convinced that a "stray U.S. Navy Cruise missile blew up the TWA [jet]." Calling the FBI, FAA, and the NTSB "co-conspirators in a monumental cover up," he alleged that "fellow pilots did not believe mechanical failure played the slightest role in the disaster." A few weeks later, an SAS pilot in New York concurred and scoffed at the "vapor-and-spark" hypothesis." "It's more a case of smoke and mirrors," he quipped.

We may never know the truth—and not for an absence of credible evidence but in the interest of "national security," a one-size-fits-all alibi used by the U.S. to tell its biggest lies, withhold the most jarring facts, or shield its most errant deeds from public scrutiny. The inventory of deceit, falsifications, and outright evasions from the truth foisted by the government on the American people is broad and tangled:

- Unwitting American civilians and low-ranking military personnel used as guinea-pigs in radiological, biological, and chemical warfare experiments, notably MK-Ultra, a top-secret CIA project in which the agency conducted hundreds of clandestine experiments—sometimes on unwitting U.S. citizens—to assess the potential use of LSD and other drugs for mind control, information gathering and psychological torture. Though Project MK-Ultra lasted from 1953 until about 1973, details of the illicit program didn't become public in highly redacted form until 1975, during a congressional investigation into widespread illegal CIA activities within the U.S. and around the world.

- Unsuspecting African-Americans denied treatment after being infected with syphilis;
- Release by the U.S. Medical Corps of microorganisms in the New York City subway to "determine how rapidly they would spread."
- The role of CIA-trained death squads in Latin America;
- The rate and ferocity with which radiation spread across the globe following the Chernobyl nuclear disaster;
- The magnitude and aftermath of the Three Mile Island Nuclear Generating Station meltdown;
- The direct effects and long-term consequences of exposure to "Yellow Rain" and "Agent Orange" during the Vietnam War. The latter is known to have sickened more than three million people.

- The extent to which deadly fissionable material spread in the Atlantic in 1986 following the sinking of a Soviet nuclear submarine 600 miles off Bermuda. Several missile silo hatches had been forced open, and the missiles, along with the nuclear warheads they contained, were gone.
- The full details of the Iran-Contra Affair, a U.S. political scandal in which the National Security Council became involved in secret weapons transactions and other activities that either were prohibited by the U.S. Congress or violated the stated public policy of the government.
- The lies perpetrated to justify the invasion of Iraq, later of Afghanistan;
- The etiology of the Gulf War syndrome; and
- The revelation that Americans have been spied upon for years by the government.

Is the case of the ill-fated TWA flight 800 destined to join America's roster of deceptions? "Practical politics consists in ignoring facts," said American journalist Henry Adams (1838-

1918). It is not unwise to conclude that meddlesome witnesses and vexing evidence are not only ignored but often silenced. As John Pilger cautions, "Official truths are often powerful illusions;" and "Don't believe anything until it's been officially denied."

AFGHANISTAN: AMERICA'S WATERLOO

The axiom that the world's destiny rests in the hands of financiers and industrialists is never more evident than in wartime. The lords of capital and cannon merchants salivate at the prospect of conflict and the prosecution of war. They laugh all the way to the bank when the first shots ring out. And no sooner do hostilities cease than they itch for another war, another golden opportunity to cry wolf and pillage the national coffers. Highly decorated Marine Corps Major General and anti-war activist Smedley Butler (1881-1940) said as much in his now-famous *War is a Racket* speech:

> "I served in all commissioned ranks from sec-
> ond lieutenant to Major General. And during
> that period I spent most of my time being a
> high-class muscle man for Big Business, for
> Wall Street, and for the bankers. In short, I was
> a racketeer for capitalism. I suspected I was just
> part of the racket all the time. Now I am sure of
> it."

And so, military transports will keep bringing
home body bags and flag-draped caskets.
Posthumous medals will be cast to honor
young people who die or go insane or commit
suicide when the nausea of blood, gore, and
the futility of unwinnable wars overcomes
them. Bugles will play taps and 21-gun salutes
will ring out in the grief-stricken stillness of a
hundred cemeteries. And, now dubbed the
focal point of the interminable and dead-end
"war on terrorism," Afghanistan, remote, immense, wild, and inhospitable—better known
as "the graveyard of empires"—will continue
to thwart efforts to "pacify," "domesticate,"
and "democratize" by military means an en-
clave throbbing with xenophobia and religious
fervor that will forever resist pacification, do-
mestication and democratization.

♦

It was in 330 BCE that Alexander the Great, trying to conquer Afghanistan, faced his fiercest battles and suffered his greatest losses. He gave up after four years. The first and second Anglo-Afghan Wars ended in a disastrous defeat for the British, first in 1842, then in 1879. A third attempt to spread British influence in the region as the First World War raged on, met with irreversible setbacks. The Russians invaded Afghanistan in 1979. They endured a nine-year calamitous conflict that resulted in catastrophic losses in men and matériel. Five years after invading Afghanistan, they became bogged down in a guerrilla war of increasing ferocity. They failed to reduce the insurgency or win acceptance by the Afghan people. Instead, Afghan resistance grew bolder and gained unanimous popular support. Fighting gradually spread to all parts of Afghanistan. Soviet airfields, garrisons, and lines of communication were ultimately disabled.

A "sanitized" document released by the U.S. Directorate of Intelligence tallies Soviet losses at "roughly 25,000 casualties, with 600 helicopters and fixed-wing aircraft, and thousands of armored vehicles and trucks destroyed. We estimate casualties in the Afghan Army at about 67,000 and insurgent casualties at some 40,000, not including civilian sympathizers." The Soviet program to transform Afghanistan into a reliable client-state failed. So did efforts to indoctrinate the Afghan people through the media as most are illiterate, suspicious of all foreigners, fanatically religious, and wed to unshakable ancestral values and traditions. Temporary if tepid demonstrations of loyalty and short-lived truces were obtained through bribery and deception (a subterfuge the U.S. has admitted using) — then lost.

♦

Napoleon's vast army's debacle on the frozen steppes of Russia in 1812, historians agree, was the result of a fundamental error in judgement: A juggernaut is no match for the bravery, selflessness, grit, and determination of a patriotic people, no matter how outnumbered they might be. In exile on Elba and reflecting on his losses before escaping, reconstituting his army, and taking on the Duke of Wellington, Napoleon quipped: "A leader has the right to be defeated, but never to be surprised." He was both surprised and soundly defeated at Waterloo.

W. E. Gutman

More than a century later, a mediocre would-be artist and budding megalomaniac, Alois Schicklgruber—better known as Adolf Hitler—who chose surprise over the prophetic lessons of history, emulated Napoleon and invaded Russia. "General Winter," the same redoubtable and invincible military tactician that decimated France's Imperial Army (Napoleon lost more than half a million men) and the heroism of Russian soldiers made short shrift of the Führer's best units. The mighty Wehrmacht was not equipped for winter warfare. Frostbite and disease cause more casualties than combat. The dead and wounded had already reached 155,000 in the first three weeks of fighting. By the end of the offensive, more than 3.5 million German soldiers had perished.

The war in Afghanistan, while vastly different from the Napoleonic and German campaigns against Russia will ultimately be lost owing a dynamic common to both: The U.S. is fighting against a well-organized, disciplined, and fiercely patriotic enemy who knows and controls the terrain and who, like quicksilver, scatters and disappears into the innumerable chasms, furrows, an crevices that cleave Afghanistan's vast mountainous terrain. Unwavering and deeply rooted religious convictions, a passionate love of country, and an abhorrence of foreign influences, which they regard as insufferable meddling and subjugation, give the Afghans added leverage and the upper hand. The proposed increase in U.S. troops is music to the ears of bankers, military contractors, and Wall Street but it can only retard, not forestall what looms as an inevitable, costly, and humiliating defeat.

Long since dead, Osama bin Laden has been elevated to symbolic eminence. His message and his mission continue to inspire and galvanize Muslims around the world. It is only when the U.S. awakens from its mythical delusions of grandeur and moral superiority, when it begins to see the world through less myopic and arrogant eyes, that the world can relax long enough to chance what could be the beginning of a meaningful dialogue between a nation long perceived as an imperialist bully and the rest of humanity. Self-deluded optimists and incurable saber-rattlers call the war in Afghanistan, now in its seventeenth year, "a stalemate." No. It's nothing short of an irreversible rout

JUSTICE:
WHEN THE BLINDFOLD COMES OFF

He stood before his accusers, bloated and worn out, a man of hefty dimensions diminished by defeat and foreboding. The man: Hermann Göring, World War I ace, Nazi Reischsmarschall, Luftwaffe chief, and morphine addict. The place: The Nuremberg trials of 1945. Robbing the world of an execution, he would commit suicide a year later. During his imprisonment, awaiting the verdict, a brooding Göring would often ruminate on the nature of war and the dynamics that trigger and sustain it.

"Naturally, the common people don't want war," he said. "But let's face it, it's the leaders of a country who determine the polity, and it's always a simple matter to drag people along, whether it's a democracy or a fascist autocracy, or a parliament, or a communist dictatorship. Voice or no voice, the people can always be brought to the bidding of the leaders. This is easy. All you have to do is to tell them they're being attacked, then denounce the pacifists for their lack of patriotism and for exposing the country to danger. It works the same in every country."[8]

The quote does not appear in transcripts of the Nuremberg trials. Although Göring spoke these words during the proceedings, he did not offer them in his testimony. These musings were made privately to Gustave Gilbert, a German-speaking American intelligence officer and psychologist. Gilbert kept a journal of his observations of the proceedings and of his conversations with prisoners, which he later published in the book, *Nuremberg Diary*. The quote is part of a chat Gilbert had with a dejected Göring in his cell on the evening of April 18, 1946, as the trials were halted for a three-day Easter recess. Göring, an educated

---

[8] A stratagem not lost on Donald J. Trump.

man, may have intuitively quoted a more ancient caveat:

> *"Beware the leader who beats the drums of war in order to whip the citizenry into a patriotic frenzy, for patriotism is a double-edged sword. It may embolden the blood, but it also cripples the mind. And when the drums of war have reached a fever pitch and the blood boils with hatred and the mind has shut down, the leader will have no need to seize the rights of the citizenry. Rather, the citizenry, infused with fear and blinded by patriotism, will offer up all their rights unto the leader, and gladly so. How do I know? For this is what I have done. I am Caesar."* [9]

Apocryphal or real, Caesar's admonitions against political leaders who all too eagerly send the young marching off to war by fabricating crises that purportedly threaten "national security" and appeal to the dementedly patriotic, sound eerily familiar in their contemporary context. In Göring's case, the sentiment expressed is disturbing because it comes not from a revered figure of antiquity, but from a reviled 20th century monster. Sure-

---

[9] Ibid.

ly, no one would doubt that an icon of classical Rome understood, more than two thousand years ago, that men can be merrily led to slaughter by their leaders. One may be forgiven for wondering whether such elementary truth has been lost on the now overstuffed and apathetic "flower children" of my youth and the clueless, self-absorbed space cadets of today's generation.

The Caesar quote, it turns out, is a latter-day fabrication by a quipster with a keen understanding of human nature. The words attributed to Göring are real. He was one of the highest-ranking Nazis in Hitler's inner circle of psychopaths. He was captured, put on trial, and found guilty of war crimes, crimes against peace, and crimes against humanity. He was sentenced to death by hanging. He took his own life with smuggled potassium cyanide capsules hours before his execution.

What Göring did not concede, at least not publicly, is that war inevitably exhausts the "common people" on both sides — not to mention the combatants. Eventually, angst turns to impatience and impatience gives way to vexation when civilians and soldiers alike realize they were counseled in the name of some absurd grand design. Nor could the Führer's right-hand man have predicted that the Nuremberg trials, magnificently run by the U.S., would culminate in the formation of an International Court of Justice that would be called upon to prosecute and punish latter-day war criminals — the intellectual authors of war-related atrocities, as well as their agents.

How many Americans would face the wrath and judgment of the international tribunal? Several administration officials, members of Congress. "undercover" operators, and men in uniform, past and present, come to mind who would find themselves in dire straits but for the fact that the U.S. has spurned the court and refused to recognize its standards and protocols (even though it attempts to corrupt those nations that do by offering them foreign aid).

The American Servicemembers' Protection Act was introduced by Senator Jesse Helms as an amendment to the Defense Authorization Act and passed in 2002 by the Bush administration. The stated purpose of the amendment was "to protect U.S. military personnel, and elected and appointed government officials against criminal prosecution by an international criminal court to which the U.S. is not a party." The amendment is intended to weaken the International Court in The Hague as it allows the U.S. government to save U.S. citizens from extradition, and also authorizes "any necessary action," as Helms put it, "to free U.S. soldiers improperly handed over to that court."

When it comes to the spirit and letter of justice, and given a long history of human rights abuses and war crimes during the Mexican American War; the Philippine American War; World War II; the Korean War (the No Gun Ri massacre); the "War on Terror" ("extraordinary rendition" and "enhanced interrogation techniques"); the Iraq War (Abu Ghraib tortures and prisoner abuses, the Mahmudiya and Haditha killings, and the Hamdania incident); and the War in Afghanistan (Bagram torture sprees and prisoner abuse, the Kandahar massacre, and the Maywand District killings) does the inelegant and persistent snub by the U.S. of a world body that picks up where the Nuremberg trials left off suggest that Americans are the butt of a colossal and habitual deception?

"There is a higher court than courts of justice," said Mahatma Gandhi, "the court of conscience. It supersedes all other courts." How can justice prevail — or be enforced — where conscience is in such meager supply?

WHAT NEXT, BOOK BURNINGS?

The First Amendment provides the best legal protection of free expression. As a result, people don't think censorship exists in America. Indeed, compared to some countries where journalists are routinely harassed, imprisoned, or worse, the Fourth Estate has weathered the meddlesome hostility and occasional threats of irate administrations with commendable poise. But this doesn't mean that speech is free. Reporters still risk jail time for refusing to disclose the identity of confidential sources. They face censorship or sacking if their accounts clash with a publication's "editorial philosophy" (doublespeak for "let's not antagonize our readers or alienate our advertisers") even intimidation and maltreatment if their accounts — or tough adversarial questions — fail to harmonize with the sloganeering claptrap uttered by the president at a press conference.[10]

Less extreme infringements on free speech occur on a daily basis, often well below the radar screen. A sixth-grader in California was charged with sexual harassment for bringing her copy of Judy Blum's *Forever* to school to lend to a friend. The friend showed it to another student, who read excerpts to a group of children during recess. The teacher confiscated the book and filed charges against the student

---

[10] Following heated sparring with President Trump at a Nov. 7, 2018 press conference, CNN chief White House correspondent Jim Acosta's press pass and U.S. Secret Service security credentials facilitating entry onto the White House grounds, were suspended "until further notice." This gross abuse of executive power has since been widely condemned. One New York Times reader wrote: "The revocation of Jim Acosta's press credentials by the White House is the act of a banana republic dictatorship. To deny press credentials to a well-known, legitimate reporter for no other reason than that the president doesn't like his questions is unprecedented in the U.S. and reveals the autocratic intentions of this president."

who brought the book to school, even though she had not witnessed the reading. The teacher argued that the book was "like a loaded gun." School administrators backed off the sexual harassment charge but still pursued disciplinary action against the student. The matter was quietly dropped when the New York-based National Coalition Against Censorship intervened, asking the school to provide legal justification for its action.

The incident never made the news. The student returned to school as if nothing had happened—the optimal result. However, for students aware of the incident, *Forever* will always be associated with the censorious attitude of school officials. Kids will think twice before they bring a book to school to lend a friend. The take-home lesson: Some issues are off limits. You're not supposed to be interested in these issues. And you're forbidden to tell anyone that you are. *Forever* was soon after removed from all school libraries in Pasadena, Texas. Books by Isabel Allende, Toni Morrison, Richard Wright, Barbara Kingsolver, E. R. Frank, Rudolph Anaya, and Lois Lowry were also pulled off the shelves in other states. Hundreds more are being impugned, some for their erotic content, others for challenging dearly held political and religious views.

Such onslaught against academic freedom and free inquiry may not rise to the level of incarceration of retaliatory "fatwah," but the cumulative effect undermines the value placed on reading and the acquisition of knowledge. This creates a framework for a national policy designed to suppress information deemed "inappropriate," "profane," or "unpatriotic" by certain groups who would, should they so be empowered, rule from the pulpit. Capricious attempts to put a chill on freedom of expression, creativity, and dissent through the use of blackjack tactics, continue to find fertile ground in an Amerika now hijacked by the right. To wit:

- The House of Representatives garnered bipartisan support for a bill that would raise from $32,000 to $500,000 the top fines for broadcast "indecency." The fines would apply to commentators, talk show hosts, musicians, and filmmakers. Which is worse? A fleeting glimpse of Janet Jackson's nipple or Armstrong Williams hyping a government program without disclosing that he was paid $240,000 to tout rapacious administration policies? What is worse, a sonorous expletive or a phony news report by a pseudo-journalist and White House toady (Jeff Gannon) about Medicare?

- PBS was railroaded into pulling an episode of the children's show, *Postcards from Buster*, when then Education Secretary, Margaret Spellings, complained that in a certain segment, Buster, a rabbit, learns how sugar maple is made in Vermont at the home of children with two female parents.

- Calling it "anti-American and anti-military," city council members in Lakewood, Colorado, removed an artwork by Air Force veteran Gayla Lemke in which she quotes Ben Franklin, i.e., "There was never a good war or a bad peace."

- Under attack for language depicting the realities of racism, the historical book, *War Comes to Willy Freeman*, by James Collier, was removed by the principal from a middle school in Ithaca, New York, even though it had been taught for ten years.

- In Portland, Oregon, Douglas County commissioners asked the museum to remove a display of the pagan goddess Hebe from a historical exhibit when some visitors complained that paganism is offensive.

♦

We don't put people in jail for what they write or think—yet. But we grimly manipulate their thoughts by controlling or dictating what they may or may not read. Other civilized nations react to this aberration with astonishment, if not consternation.

"How can this happen in a country that purports to embrace free speech," a French academic asked me recently. I said nothing. The question was the answer. I shrugged my shoulders and smiled. After all, had I not brought to school some seventy years ago an oddball assortment of items for show-and-tell—my two-headed pet turtle Janus, an exquisitely explicit anatomical atlas, my father's gynecological speculum, and an illustrated copy of the Marquis de Sade's Justine—without incurring the wrath of my teachers or fearing that I might bring it upon myself?

Of course, I was about ten and living in decadent Europe, not upstanding America. Now an octogenarian, I find it a great paradox that a nation that has honed promiscuity to an art can be, or pretend to be, so puritanical, so righteous. But that's another story.

A First Amendment is not enough. People have to understand it, believe in it, and fiercely protect it. Freedom of expression is not just a fundamental right, it's also an essential characteristic of an intellectually emancipated, enlightened, well informed society.

The greatest obstacle to knowledge is not ignorance but the illusion that we know it all.

FROM HOAX TO HOLY RELIC

An air of pious exultation wafts over the elegant Baroque city of Turin, Italy. Its most illustrious artifact: The Shroud, which some Christians believe is Jesus' burial cloth and an artifact that despite its questionable authenticity, continues to feed the ecstatic character of Catholicism.

The winding sheet bears the likeness of an old bearded man with long scraggly hair, which some Christians assert is Jesus. It was repaired in 2002 to remove a patch woven by 16th century nuns after a small portion of the cloth was damaged by fire. Many respected scholars contest the shroud's authenticity. Most believe it was produced in the Middle Ages when purported biblical-era vestiges, including splinters from the cross, suddenly popped up across Europe. According to church historian Antonio Lombatti, "the owner of the shroud said in 1355 that the local bishop called it a forgery and that even the pope [Innocent VI] said it was fake."

A piece of fabric of questionable provenance and disputed vintage hardly establishes anyone's historicity. It confirms, at best, the ancient Jewish custom of burying the dead in a shroud and a simple pine casket, a tradition observed to this day by Jews who reject the flamboyance of modern funerals.

The imprint of a human form on a piece of cloth produced by biochemical reactions does not provide scientific proof that the image is Jesus' any more than the claim that he was "raised from the dead," a fantastical assertion that defies logic (unless he wasn't dead in the first place) and has no more basis in fact than the zany conspiratorial theory that he, his wife Marie-Magdalene, and their brood fled to southern France where they proceeded to found the Merovingian royal dynasty.

Hard as I try, I fail to see how a tale woven of pure cloth [pun intended] "demonstrates the human potential to conquer death," as some Church diehards claim—a feat never duplicated before or since— and that clearly violates natural laws, not to mention the fact that the image on the shroud is that of a very old and very dead man well past his thirty-third birthday. If I accurately quote from the lexicon of Christian mythology, "transubstantiation" refers to "the change from bread and wine to the body and blood of Christ." There is nothing in ancient Hebrew and Aramaic texts to suggest that Jesus ever exclaimed, "This bread is my body," etc. This would have been terribly "un-Jewish" on his part. This fabrication was added by overzealous scribes who, through the ages, shamelessly redacted "inconvenient" or "politically incorrect" chronicles and added improbable scenarios that owe their longevity to blind faith in mind-boggling fantasy.

Undeterred by science-fact, unmoved by reason, the Church, which commands *Credo ad Absurdum*—believe because it is absurd— then insists that the science-fiction-like metamorphoses can also result in photo-luminescence.

Using electron microscopy and X-ray diffraction, the late Dr. Walter McCrone, a leading expert in microscopy, found red ochre (iron oxide, hematite) and vermilion (mercuric sulfide) on the shroud. The electron microscope analyzer detected iron, mercury, and sulfur on a dozen of the blood-image area samples of the shroud. The results fully confirmed Dr. McCrone's suspicions that the image was painted twice, once with red ochre, followed by vermilion to enhance the blood-image areas. Late results of carbon dating at three laboratories corroborated Dr. McCrone's earlier findings: The shroud is a haunting painting created in the mid-14th century for a new church sorely in need of a pilgrim-baiting attraction. The suggestion that fire had singed a small portion of cloth could have altered the chemical character of the entire shroud, thus rendering it less authentic, is ludicrous.

The Catholic Church's official position is as transparent as it is dismissive. Christianity's most cherished relic is an indispensable "tool" for faith; its authenticity is irrelevant. The former archbishop of Turin, Cardinal Severino Poletto, has urged the flock to "gaze upon the shroud with your eyes rather than your minds."

Jesus, the consummate radical who abhorred all forms of idolatry, would have a fit if he knew how his teachings degenerated into faith by symbolism, superstition, and subterfuge.

RELIGION: A FORM OF PSYCHOSIS?

I reread the item three times out loud just to make sure I wasn't hallucinating. Datelined Rome, February 11, 2008, it crowed:

> "The 150th anniversary of the apparition in Lourdes of the Virgin Mary was marked by a procession that culminated at St. Peter's Basilica, Christianity's most hallowed edifice, where a rib of Bernadette Soubirous, revered by the Church and blessed by the Pope as a saintly relic, was placed on display before an adoring crowd of worshippers."

A rib, a macabre artifact idolized not in some antediluvian corner of the world but in Italy where the Renaissance was born and the seeds of Enlightenment were first sown! That such ghoulish buffoonery should take place in the 21st century, I protested, is both pathetic and alarming.

Suspended midway between waning faith and reason, a friend wistfully suggested that "people need religion; societies would collapse without it." Coming to his senses, he added: "Of course, the more sorcery and theatrics religion delivers, the more believable and persuasive its teachings become." I agree that the fiendish mechanics my friend described make religion more alluring but I reject the notion that people "need" religion or that some apocalyptic meltdown would occur without it. Religion is a syllabus in which are cast ironclad proscriptions and commands, threats, weird forebodings, and penalties enforced with incantations and histrionics that the faithful are encoded to regard as essential to their earthly lives and spiritual well-being. Faith is a potent narcotic, but only those who have been "turned on," generally by force from infancy, succumb to its lethal "high." People are not genetically inclined to embrace it. Nor do they innately acquire an urge to submit. One does not become a junkie until one has sampled the toxic, addictive merchandise. Religious beliefs are neither the product of evolutionary instincts nor a choice. They are first infused in an unsullied psyche then reinforced through repetition, the promise of redemption, and the discipline of fear. Nor does religion prevent violence or promote morality and ethical conduct. Morality predates religion by millennia. Cultural anthropologists have shown that even the most "primitive" societies live under codes of behavior that are not religious in origin, scope, or intent. Conversely, history has demonstrated time after time that copious amounts of blood were shed in the name of "God" and that it continues to be spilled in modern sectarian conflicts and individual acts of religious hatred. In contrast, I cannot recall a single war being waged in the name of atheism.

I also challenge the assertion that mankind would wander in a spiritual desert without "divine" guidance. I was brought up in an ambience utterly devoid of religion. An absence of casual or ritualistic spirituality at home did not create a void in my life and, as I tell anyone willing to listen, I found the notion of an omnipotent, ineffable, unknowable creator/judge/destroyer preposterous even as a child. [I did learn how to deny being a Jew in half a dozen languages when I lived in German-occupied France). Yes, I went through my "mystical period," immersing myself in the study of the Tao, Zen, Tantric Buddhism, Sikhism, as well as Judaism, Christianity, and Islam. Like my father before me, I'd spent countless hours "meandering in stupefied fascination" through the Kabbalah's cerebral minefields. The hurdles of comprehension, not to mention the surreal leaps of faith the Kabbalah demands, would leave me exhausted and perplexed, not enlightened. However enthralling, my side trips to the far ends of reason were inspired by the urge to know, not a need to belong or partake. Eventually, I concluded that "God" is a useless and costly hypothesis with which I could dispense.

As children we accept without hesitation the "realities" that our parents, educators, and "spiritual" shepherds promote—from Santa Claus to the bogeyman and the tooth fairy, from the existence of a supernatural Übermensch to the virgin birth of a rabble-rouser whose alleged teachings and those of his followers were conflated into a new religion more than three hundred years after his death. We quickly learn that Santa, the bogeyman, and the tooth fairy are myth and fraud. Yet, with sufficient parental encoding, which includes crafty counsel not to wander beyond the limits of the "realities" they espouse, and punctuated by the constant drumbeat of religious indoctrination, we enter adulthood fully conditioned to accept—and keep alive—absurdities that owe their existence and longevity, to blind faith.

It was Sigmund Freud who postulated the now widely accepted theory that we are the product of our subconscious. But he was careful to add that the "subconscious" is not an amorphous and indelible entity; it's the end-product of countless dynamics, the least of which is genetic. Our subconscious is molded, fashioned, and often perverted by early childhood experiences, some of them traumatic, and by brainwashing (the planting of immovable ideas) by parents, teachers, clergy, and other figures of authority. No one is "born" a believer or an atheist. No one comes out of the womb a Liberal or a Conservative. Serial killers and good Samaritans are made, not sired. The subconscious mind can be manipulated and controlled for both good and evil. Religion has been a master manipulator, with Christianity hoodwinking the flock with charades that range from paganism and idolatry (worshipping statues) to vampirism and cannibalism (Communion) to a descent into terminal psychosis (the belief of life after death). All monotheistic religions are inherently violent. Neither Judaism nor Islam is exempt from criticism. Laws requiring the eradication of "evil," sometimes by violent means, exist in the Jewish tradition. Yahweh is a jealous, cruel, and vindictive "God." Allah" the Merciful," too, is formidable, strict, and wrathful. Mainstream Islamic law is riddled with detailed calls for violence, defensive or offensive, including the use of aggression within the family or household, the use of corporal and capital punishment, as well as how, when, and against whom to wage war.

In the philosophy of religion, Occam's razor of parsimony is sometimes applied to argue the existence or non-existence of "God." While it does not attempt to disprove it, it offers a compelling argument that, in the absence of convincing reasons to believe in deity, disbelief should be preferred. I disagree with those who suggest that Occam's razor compares apples and oranges. Instead, it illustrates with blinding clarity that while, say, Christianity has branched into often dissimilar and almost always bickering factions—each defiantly claiming that it alone has direct access to "God"—atheism, given its axiomatic simplicity and honesty, has not changed. A lack of belief cannot be codified. There are no Orthodox, Conservative, or Reform atheists. Atheists have no "holy book, catechism, or psalters. All speak in the single voice of reason. No schism can splinter us. Nor are we in the least interested in defending our ideas as are religious people doggedly determined to convince others of the validity (and divine origin) of their beliefs. An atheist is quite content not to believe; a believer feels compelled to "share," perhaps as a way of validating his faith by fanning away the ever-present whiffs of doubt that consume all believers.

Religion, by its very nature, clings to fictions that do not exist in the absolute vacuum of pure thought; instead, they must be "planted" in the mind so they may burgeon. i.e., "God" is the source of all essence and reality; Jesus was the son of "God;" he was born to a virgin; he rose from the dead; his death and rebirth open a portal to eternal life. Whoever or whatever he was, man or myth, Jesus opposed formal religion, abhorred the mix of politics and worship (think Israel and Muslim theocracies), and held the self-aggrandizing bluster of believers in contempt.

Atheism warns against the tyranny of absolutist ideas, not hell and eternal damnation. It promises no redemption other that freedom from absurd beliefs. It offers no indulgences or exemptions from sin in exchange for bribes; it has no pontiff and no Church in which crimson-clad "princes" live in Babylonian splendor; no avaricious plate-passing beadles; it delivers no sermons; it issues no threats of fire and brimstone, holy war, and cataclysms; it neither warns of eternal agony nor promises a bliss-filled afterlife. Atheists do not burn books. They do not have an Index of prohibited works. They have no need for a Congregation for the Doctrine of the Faith [formerly known as the Holy Office of the Inquisition) which, by its very existence, demonstrates the perilous fragility of religion. Last, atheists, seldom spontaneously but after much internal turmoil and self-inquiry, conclude that there is no "God" and that, therefore, human beings are neither created nor imbued with anything that can have a plan or idea as to what they will be like before they come into existence or before they develop by their own free action. Atheism is simple, clear, and straightforward.

Even at the height of man's most primitive existence — think "prehistory" — Homo sapiens lived by rules and codes of behavior geared to create a cohesive social order. And when they gazed heavenward, terrified by lightning and thunder, they were cowed by a fear of the unknown, not by a single, invisible but all-powerful spirit. Papua New Guinea and patches of dense Amazonian forest, the last bastions of stone-age societies {many of them since forced into Christianity] practice Animism, a belief system based on all things, including animals, inanimate objects, plants, and rocks to which they ascribe a life of their own. They also observe codes of behavior that continue to baffle and inspire social anthropologists. Absent from their vocabulary, for example, are words or concepts that all too often define modern man, including cheating, stealing, hatred, and other traits commonly frowned upon in the west where they have been honed to an art. The fact that they consider their lives fated by their ancestors, by the wind, the rain, the sun, and the fauna and flora in whose bosom they live in exquisite harmony, does not in any way suggest the existence of a formal religion.

Religion is learned, not innate or intuitive. An addict needs his fix because he indulged in addictive drugs in the first place. An alcoholic purchased his disease in a liquor store; he wasn't born with it. One does not "get" religion except through a subtle and gradual osmosis. I would argue that people who are never exposed to religion will not suddenly develop an urge to embrace absurd beliefs without the intervention of some powerful and persuasive medium. Religion may have "tamed" some people but it has also poisoned the soul of many and led to intolerance and horrific inhumanity.

The conversion of the Aztec, Maya, and Inca, first under the menacing sword and coercive force of the cross brandished by their Majesties' Catholic Conquistadores, and their descendants by hordes of Protestant missionaries, was carried out with cunning patience and a perseverance akin to fanaticism. It is the promise of food, shelter, and decent healthcare that propels millions of poor and culturally alienated indigenous groups around the world to the baptismal pool, not the irrepressible urge to abandon their ancestral traditions in exchange for alien concepts and systems of belief.

♦

We are all born with a blank slate. Only parental rearing and the societal pressures mold us into cookie-cutter replicas of our would-be retrofitters. We are all initially endowed with a brain capable of discerning the truth but now so badly mangled by encoding and rote repetition that we succumb to ritualistic, synchronous reflex that, we are programmed to believe, benefits us and "society."

Yes, we are the stuff that stars are made of. We are the product of eons of fusion. But "fusion" implies only the amalgamation and compacting of disparate elements. Man's parts are infinitely larger and more diverse that his whole, and it is the parts that result in geniuses and idiots, assassins and philanthropists, creators and social parasites, adventurers, human dynamos, and couch potatoes, loving parents and infanticidal monsters.

♦

I harbor no animosity toward the "faithful." What I resent and dread is the fury of evangelism, the obstinate zeal of proselytism. My aim has never been to convince others of the non-existence of "God." My objective, if I can call it so, is to encourage a dialogue which has as its central theme the proposition that atheism is as much a product of "revelation" — scientific empiricism and common sense — as is the claim that the existence of a "Grand Architect of the Universe" is revealed. Underlying that aim is the hope that radical and absolute separation between Church and State can be achieved which, while in no way curtailing religious freedoms, leads to a secular society guided by and devoted to reason and free thought.

We are witnessing the first blossoms in the rebirth of reason as large numbers of people are now leaving the faith tradition of their up-bringing or abandoning religion altogether. Alas, rising anti-Semitism, Islamophobia, and the sporadic persecution of Sikhs and Christians place in sharp focus the sanguinary character of religion and the evil scale of human hatred.

THE MAGNIFICENT MARQUIS

I have no heroes, alive or dead. Other than my late father, an iron-willed, incorruptible man and dedicated physician, I admire few people—in or out of the limelight. It takes an exceptional blend of intellect, talent, creativity, integrity, kindness, charisma, and the high regard of posterity to earn a person the lasting legacy of "admirability." Descartes, Spinoza, Mozart and Beethoven, Lincoln, Martin Luther King, and Gandhi, Albert Schweitzer and Father Damien are among my chosen few. This reverence for genius, moral fiber, and altruism, however, does not prevent me from granting a measure of esteem for less than perfect men who, navigating the dark, shark-infested waters of ignorance, superstition, and fear, manage to alter their nation's character and destiny. Inevitably, when I think of these men, I also imagine how nations hopelessly mired in corruption and ineptitude, or those currently losing their grip on democracy, would benefit from their ideas, skills, and strength of character—were they still alive today.

One such, almost fictional, oddball, little known outside the Iberian Peninsula, is the controversial 18th century reformer, Sebastiâo José de Carvalho e Mello, better known as the Marquis of Pombal, the virtual leader of the kingdom of Portugal at a time of turmoil and sectarian bloodshed, and considered by the Portuguese as their greatest statesman. The marquis' crowning achievement is the disbandment of the Inquisition in Portugal and later in Spain, and the introduction of administrative, educational, cultural, economic, and ecclesiastical reforms justified in the name of "reason"—a heretical concept the almighty Church despised and feared. He was instrumental is advancing secularism and promoting a free press at a time when the "Holy" Inquisition barbecued people for having had a Jewish or Muslim ancestor, or for uttering inconvenient truths.

Having lived in Vienna and London, the latter city in particular being a major center of the Enlightenment, de Pombal increasingly believed that the Jesuits, with their grip on science and education, were an obstacle to an independent, Portuguese-style democratic *illuminismo*. Given that the Jesuits were the chief inquisitors in Portugal, de Pombal's efforts against them greatly weakened and eventually loosened the Inquisition's grip in Europe and the Colonies. Undoubtedly the most prominent prime minister of Portugal, he is considered to have been the de facto head of an absolute monarchy. Notable for his swift action and leadership in the aftermath of the devastating 1755 earthquake that leveled Lisbon and killed an estimated 110,000 people, he implemented sweeping economic policies to regulate commercial activity and standardize manufacturing quality control.

De Pombal's greatest reforms were economic and financial, with the creation of several companies and professional guilds. He ruled with a heavy hand, imposing the strict equality of law on all citizens, from the high nobility to the working class. These reforms earned him enemies in the upper classes, especially among aristocrats and members of the clergy who reviled him as a social upstart, a heretic, and a gadfly. In 1759, he expelled the Jesuits who had a stranglehold on education. He instituted a secular public primary and secondary school system, introduced vocational training, created hundreds of new teaching posts, added departments of mathematics and natural science to the University of Coimbra, and introduced new taxes to pay for these reforms. Even the Vatican reluctantly concedes that, *"in the political sphere [de Pombal's] administration was marked by boldness of conception and tenacity of purpose. He leveled all classes, imposed absolute obedience to the law, which was largely decided by himself because the tribunals had long ceased to function, and he transformed the Inquisition into an insignificant and largely impotent arm of the State."* His most notable legislative work includes the abolition of Indian slavery, putting an end to the persecution of Jews, and declaring them full-fledged citizens of Portugal. He restructured Portugal's finances, reformed the army and navy, and founded the School of Commerce and the Royal Press.

♦

Fear of enlightenment during the Inquisition, as it is today in the U.S., was such that censorship—by intimidation, persecution, and indifference to human suffering—became the main preoccupation of the ruling elite. Then and now, scholars saw the curtailment of knowledge and free thought, and the concentration of power and wealth in a handful of plutocrats as being responsible for the growing intellectual decrepitude of society.

Of course, no one is being burned at the stake but a form of inquisition still festers—the immovable socio-economic, and cultural vice-like grip on the masses by a small minority of immensely rich individuals. Equally deplorable is the absence of men (or women) with the Marquis of Pombal's credentials, temperament, and progressive vision.

Some readers will call the foregoing three hundred-year rearward leap in time trivial or its insinuations and conclusions inapplicable to the present. I disagree. The past has always been prologue and an immovable past is a sure recipe for disaster. Added to verifiable fact, trivia is invaluable. It puts meat on the bone of history. It also warns hooligans and profiteers that posterity is watching.

WHERE HAVE THE
FLOWER CHILDREN GONE?

History, culture, and tradition drive national values. In some countries, these values are so deeply ingrained that conventions, rituals, and loyalties become embedded in the national psyche.

Seventy-three years after Hiroshima and Nagasaki, Japan is waxing nostalgic. It is looking at its youth, hedonistic, hopelessly seduced by the West's tawdriest trappings, and pining for an era when Bushido, the Honor Code of the Warrior, governed every aspect of life. In its purest form, Bushido elevates fearlessness, justice, benevolence, and honesty. It also demands of its disciples that they look backward at the present from the moment of their own death—as if they were already dead. Bushido, in effect, is the path to an honorable life. The Bushido of the Samurai was the spiritual basis for those who undertook kamikaze missions during World War II.

On April 12, 1945, Lt. Shinichi Uchida faced a terrifying mission—crash his plane into a U.S. warship. The young kamikaze's final letter to his grandparents was full of bravado:

"Now I'll go and get rid of those devils," the 18-year-old pilot wrote shortly before his final flight. He was never seen again.

For many, such rhetoric is redolent of the militarism and fierce chauvinism that drove Japan to ruin. But for an increasingly bold cadre of conservatives, Uchida's words symbolize something else: the kind of guts and commitment, the "divine wind" that today's Japanese youth seem to lack. No one is publicly calling for young Japanese to kill themselves for the nation these days. But the renewed hero-worship of the kamikaze coincides with a general trend in Japanese society where the moral and intellectual defection of its youth and a fading ethic of idealism are now being mourned.

The estimated 4,000 kamikaze ("divine wind") pilots were named after a legendary typhoon that foiled the Mongol emperor Kublai Khan's invasion of Japan in 1281. As many as 90 percent failed to reach the U.S. warships they were commanded to attack. Despite the pilots' reputation abroad as suicidal fanatics, Japanese hearts have always had a soft spot for the kamikaze. Long celebrated in movies, novels, and comic books, the pilots are seen as innocent young men forced by a desperate military to sacrifice their lives in order to protect their country.

In contrast, while young Americans are sacrificing their lives, limbs, and sanity in calamitous, immoral, and unwinnable wars, the self-indulgent apathy of today's "baby boomers" and "generation X" has all but obscured the exuberant effrontery and defiance of a peer group not afraid to speak up against injustice, government lies, presidential chicanery, and the sham piety of spiritual leaders.

The 1960s and 1970s ushered an era oxygenated by the rise of a lively counterculture. Emancipated from the phony puritanism of the finicky Fifties, cleansed from the obscenity of McCarthyism, sickened by the Vietnam War, the Kent massacre, and the Watergate Scandal, America welcomed the Beatles, let its hair down, set fire to ROTC buildings, and donned Nehru jackets. Malcolm X spoke out with eloquence and bitterness about the black man's lot in white America. Black Panther leader Eldridge Cleaver and comedian Dick Gregory, tireless drum-majors for civil rights, parlayed acerbic tongue and mordant wit into a brand of social activism that helped bolster black America's self-identity. James Baldwin rose from obscurity to become a commanding figure in American literature. A cultural phenomenon, Alex Haley's Roots offered for the first time a black perspective of life in Africa and unerringly records the bestiality of the slave trade. In Kunta Kinté are incarnated the horrors and heroism of the black experience. Lenny Bruce, Mort Sahl, and George Carlin turned humor on its head. Their irreverence and biting satire challenged a hypocritically straitlaced society and helped redefine and broaden free speech. Jack Kerouac, the leading chronicler of the "beat generation" — he had coined the term — shocked America with autobiographical sketches that reflect deep social angst assuaged by drugs, alcohol, spiritualism, and scorching antiestablishment humor. His leading apostle, Allen Ginsberg, vented his rage against materialism with poignancy and lyricism. Flower children preached love, not war. Oh! Calcutta, memorable for its frontal nudity, male and female, and Hair, America's tribal love-rock musical, opened to rave reviews. The plays would enthrall audiences for years to come. This was an age of rebellious sex and drugs and freedom from the shackles of thoughtless, reckless convention and naiveté, a time of refreshing impiety and suspicion toward the political structures that Americans take for granted and trust, an epoch long remembered and still reviled by a conservative core that lived through it and died a little.

I remember watching these transformations with relish. I rejoiced at the consternation these upheavals wreaked on America's squeamish psyche. They filled me with hope. For a change, but ever so briefly, I was proud to be an American. I saw in the politics of open dissent the same dauntless spirit that has infused the Patriots two centuries earlier.

Where are the flower children, the rebels, the draft-card burners, the gallant conscientious objectors, and the refuseniks now that we really need them? What happened to

America's spirit now that a dictator who consciously and obstinately disregards the will of the people, is pushing America toward the brink? Why aren't million-man marches flooding the streets of America and advancing on the White House and Congress, like the ragtag band of revolutionaries did when they stormed the Bastille, to proclaim their revulsion and force the scalawags out? Why has this nation lost its will to express moral indignation?

Neutrality is a form of crass indifference further sullied by irresolution. Silence and laissez-faire are tantamount to cowardice. Cowardice promotes negligence — the criminal kind.

TRUTH vs. PEACEMAKING

Two friends were having a heated discussion the other night. Call them John and Matthew. The pair is always at each other's throat. Each resents the other's opinions with a passion only clashing egos — not scholarship or reason — can inflame. Their spats are petty, volcanic, generally brief but apt to re-ignite at the slightest provocation. John and Matthew have turned ideological ranting into a form of dialectical perpetual motion. Round and round they go, holding on for dear life to their cherished positions and, predictably, getting nowhere. Their opinions are banal; they're not grounded in fact. Ignorance is the mother of invention: When facts escape them, they make things up. It gives them presence among those who know even less. Like their Biblical name-sakes, they have no clear understanding of history, so they rewrite it, skewering reality and adding falsehoods to myths.

Both recently asked me to referee one of their tempestuous squabbles—with "left" versus "right," not fact versus opinion—at the center of their quarrel. I suggested instead that we ask two mutual friends, Luke and Mark, to arbitrate. John and Matthew agreed, confident that two judges might deliver contrasting verdicts, thus allowing the perennial protagonists to adhere to their respective positions.

"So, Matthew," asked Luke, "what's all this about?" Matthew obliged, sounding off with more vehemence than common sense.

"Well," Luke offered cautiously, "I think Matthew may have a point."

"Just a doggone minute," John griped. "Why don't you hear me out before surrendering to Matthew?"

"You're right, John," said Luke. "By all means, please proceed." Pontificating, as is his style, John told his side of the story.

"You know what," said Luke, "on second thought, I think John may be onto something."

"Hold it," I intervened. "How can both John and Matthew be right?"

Mark, who had placidly followed the debate, placed a conciliatory hand on my shoulder, looked at me in the eye and proclaimed, "Tell you what; you're right too!"

I was baffled but said nothing. Mark was not being diplomatic but a model of equivocation and frivolity. Anxious to make peace, he did the truth a disservice. As I weighed the doctrinal differences that so diametrically and pointlessly divide Mathew and John, I also pondered Mark's Solomonic ruling. Drawing from Zen, to which I turn when Western rigidity gets in the way, but careful not to become confused about the relationship between its teachings as a guide to the truth and mistaking it for the truth itself, I suddenly apprehended Mark's vacuous appeasement and disarming blow to reason. I then examined my own "convictions" and found them to be mercifully less than firm or unfailing. Depending on the issues, I allow them to oscillate from pole to pole. Those who *seek* the truth, I keep telling myself, are infinitely closer to it than those who claim to have found it. In so doing,

I grant myself the right to change my mind as often as it takes to find it.

♦

Sometimes, the only way to understand and acknowledge the scope of a problem is to confront it head-on and with an open mind. This is something that John and Matthew doggedly refuse to do. They'd rather cling to their convictions than risk being proven wrong. They stopped searching. They wrapped themselves in the security blanket of fixed ideas, shut the door tightly against the very light of knowledge, and they don't let anyone else pry it open. Luke is impartial and generous but he wavers. Mark makes the astute connection between apparent truth and incontrovertible fact, between irresistible force and immovable object. But he solves nothing.

"Right," like "wrong," is what the self perceives. What we perceive, however, is seldom shaped by irrefutable reality or truth but by conditioning. Often, what we choose to believe is born of an unwillingness to go beyond the obvious. Inflexible ideas are the offspring of intellectual sloth. They are the enemies of truth. The truths that others have come to grasp intuitively can never become ours unless we come to understand them through our own mental efforts. Each of us has a different way of reaching the same destination. There isn't just one road, and not everyone is fit to travel the same course. By limiting our journey to a single trail, we may actually be leading ourselves astray.

G. K. Chesterton (1874-1936), English poet, writer, philosopher, lay theologian, and rabid anti-Semite, was wrong. Heretics are not "those who pride themselves in their superiority to conventional views." They are free-thinking people who are willing to question conventional doctrine and faith-based edicts, and have the moral courage to examine the validity of their own beliefs.

The worst thing we can do is go around and spread our own adopted superficialities. Ignorance, of which idle knowledge is one aspect, is the root cause of friction among men. We should all be more interested in truth than in peacemaking at any cost, especially the inconvenient kind

SHOOTING THE MESSENGER

A central argument in *Antigone*, a play by Sophocles (496-405 B.C.) in which is uttered the famous epigram, *"No one likes the bearer of bad news,"* is the right of the individual to reject society's infringements, to tally them, expose them, and condemn them.

Journalists and whistleblowers have one thing in common: They're perceived as arrogant, insensitive, and vexing meddlers. Their disclosures are seldom appreciated. Both seek the truth, one in the interest of history, the other in the service of justice. Both are vital cogs in the vast and complex machine that energizes free societies. They become indispensable when democracy is trivialized and threatened by deliberate myopia, lies, and unyielding beliefs.

The great and constant frustration journalists and whistleblowers endure is not with the carping of diehards and know-nothings who just like to hear the sound of their own voices but with the cowardice and perfidy of a public that chooses to remain silent out of fear, political expediency, ideological sloth, or of strategically placed individuals who engage in crypto-fascist prattle crafted to portray incorruptible and outspoken members of the press as gadflies, mudslingers, busybodies, purveyors of fake news, spreaders of social discontent, blabbermouths who threaten the established "order," and enemies of the people.

Being a gadfly and a muckraker, as I have often been called, has one notable advantage. Unlike myth-peddlers and bearers of glad tidings, gadflies are heard. Gripes get more attention than eulogies. Which is why journalism has become such a perilous occupation. For years I thought that one way of erring on the side of justice was to side unerringly with the victims of injustice—the vanquished, the persecuted, the forgotten, the dreamers. Behind prison walls. At mass graves and hurriedly dug sepulchers. Wherever voices of dissent and cries for freedom are being hushed. Amid the anonymous bones scattered about the steaming earth. Political chicanery, xenophobia, racism, pogroms, torture, war, genocide, ethnic cleansing—they'd all become a blur in an unceasing tempest of human agony.

Telling inconvenient truths is risky business, even when couched in the language of dreams. I know. I've been in the trenches as tracer bullets whizzed over my head. I've been grazed once or twice. Had my reflexes failed me when I spoke of political corruption, police brutality, and military crimes, I might not be vexing you today.

Much still begs to be unearthed, revealed, and dissected. Alas, words survive briefly in the two-dimensional realm of a book or opinion piece but they fail to generate lasting change. Instead, they leave a wasteland of rhetoric that does nothing to alter human nature, chill passions, and curb hatred. Some horrors are simply too shocking for words. Is truth-telling worth the wall of odium and discord it raises? I struggle with the question with every stroke of the pen. I keep writing. But as I do, I can envisage the day when my pen will run dry in a river of ink whose course was diverted by some fanatic in high office.

Mark my words. That day is near. The floodgates of lunacy are now wide open.

THE IRREVOCABLE RIGHT TO DIE

Being of sound mind and resolute purpose, I do herewith proclaim this to be my last will and testament, hereby revoking any and all previous wills, testaments or codicils.

Whereas I regard life as a gift and a magnificent journey, but deem it utterly without purpose or merit if degraded by old age, physical incapacitation, the loss of full mental and intellectual faculties, pain and/or irreversible disease; and

Whereas I deem physical pain neither virtuous nor ennobling but frightening, cruel and debasing; and

Whereas I believe that the "right to life" includes the unconditional right to die on one's own terms—temporal and spatial;

I hereby instruct my survivors, executors and/or caretakers to forgo any extraordinary means of resuscitation or prolongation of life by any artificial means, especially if full recovery, physical and mental, cannot be guaranteed. More specifically, if my life cannot be sustained without the aid of extended artificial respiration and/or intravenous or tubal nourishment, I direct and order that any and all such artificial life-maintaining measures be halted even if it results in death.

Wishing to leave this world as I entered it—one utterly unaware and indifferent of the other—I request that no ceremony, religious or secular, be conducted upon my death. I further request that my remains be cremated and, if circumstances allow, that my ashes be scattered—half in the Seine River, in my beloved Paris where I was born, the other half in New York Harbor, where my great American odyssey began.

I take this opportunity to express dismay at America's puritanical, hypocritical, intrusive, and self-serving views on life, euthanasia, and death, for its obscene grandstanding

and moral preening during the tragic and con-
flict-ridden Teresa Marie Schiavo case, which
was hopelessly clouded by partisan politics
and religious extremism, and to convey my
contempt for the sinister power of symbol politics. The travesty that was being played for
fifteen years while Schiavo was being kept in
an irreversible persistent vegetative state is, in
my opinion, strictly American in character,
fueled by morbid voyeurism, vulgar meddling, and the public's mistaken impression
that it was entitled to debate a strictly private
matter.

The Schiavo affair would have never made
the news in Europe. It would have been han-
dled and resolved by the family and the medical establishment. I believe the only way to
reach a sensible consensus is to personalize
this tragic fifteen-year charade: What would I
opt for if I were in a similar situation? Would I
demand that exceptional measures be taken to
keep me artificially alive? Would I insist that
an astronomical capital of time, emotion,
money, and medical technology be expended
indefinitely to keep me physiologically alive?
My answer is an emphatic NO!

Once imparted, life belongs solely and
wholly to the living. No man or institution can

abrogate this birthright. Being a freethinker and humanist, I further submit that my body and the brief span of time accorded me belong to me exclusively. Moreover, I have the right to terminate my life in the most painless and expeditious manner possible lest I linger, even for an instant, in insufferable pain and robbed of dignity.

Surely, a nation that unscrupulously sends the flower of its youth to die, be maimed or rendered insane on some distant battlefield, or executes in cold blood society's chaff, can also grant a graceful ending to those who ask for it. If gravely ill pets deserve to be "humanely" put out of their misery—and they do—the same ethos and courtesy must apply to humans.

Last, I also wish to denounce, eight years after his death, the heinous, vindictive, mind-bending faith-inspired legal persecutions to which Dr. Jack Kevorkian was subjected. Kevorkian revolutionized the concept of euthanasia by working to help people end their own suffering. He believed physicians are responsible for alleviating the suffering of patients, even if that means allowing them to die. One will never know whether his detractors acted out of moral outrage or because they felt that, if the idea caught on, the IRS would prematurely lose taxpayers, whereas houses of worship would be robbed of dues-paying sinners utterly unmoved by "God's" wrath.

♦

It was one slow, this time lethal dose of morphine that yanked my mother and maternal uncle—one was dying of pancreatic cancer, the other of multiple myeloma—from months of agonizing pain. Both believed that life loses its allure and meaning when a terminal illness threatens to cut it short. Both were mercifully liberated by caretakers who understood and respected their right to die on their own terms. Near the end, my father, a doctor who died of heart disease at eighty-three, and who understood the irrevocable nature of his condition, asked the attending physician to end his life. The physician obliged.

Saving a life is a noble endeavor. Respecting a person's right to be spared the agony of unmanageable pain or irreversible incapacitation is a sublime act of charity. Obstructing or delaying this right is the work of the devil. A merciful end is infinitely better than the endless horror of an unendurable life.

POSTSCRIPT: BEYOND THE DREAMS

Marked by time and history, the 11th century Saint-Germain-des-Près church stands proud in its austere architectural simplicity. Across the street, patrons at *Les Deux Magots* café sip fragrant espressos in thimble-sized cups and cool pale wines in fluted glasses. In their chairs once sat Ernest Hemingway and Albert Camus, Gertrude Stein and Jean-Paul Sartre, Pablo Picasso and James Joyce, to name a few. Around the corner, in a stately mansion that housed the École Supérieure de Journalisme[11], an eighteen-year-old aspiring

---

[11] Then located on Rue de Rennes, the school has long since moved to Rue de Tolbiac.

reporter listens intently to the rector's acerbic homily:

> *"You'll dissect history as if it were a corpse at a post-mortem. You'll chew on political science and sociology until your jaws hurt. You'll learn to wrest information from reticent witnesses, suppress personal biases, and dominate sentences by luxuriating in as few words as possible. We can't sell you inspiration, imagination, curiosity, skepticism, least of all the greatest of all virtues — an unconditional respect for truth and the dogged determination to exhume it, sublime and uplifting or hideous and vile, wherever it may hide."*

The rector casts a slow, sweeping look at the sea of young faces before him and adds, *"Good journalists must also have the capacity to dream, for dreaming will carry you beyond the limits of manifest reality, which is where the truth dwells."*

Uttered 65 years ago, the rector's cryptic words still echo with singular resonance. I've had my share of dreams. I also learned that reality can be strange and gruesome, that, like dreams, reality can be hard to decipher, that both are rival symptoms of the same incurable disease. Ultimately, I concluded, reality is incurable. The difference between the two is obvious only to dreamers—thinkers—for their nocturnal escapades and wakeful meditations are often the scene of untold agonies, unspoken longings, and bouts of silent fury against ignorance, stupidity, and the tyranny of coerced doctrine and inflexible beliefs.

This, in essence, has been my central and most consistent message. Implicit in my cautionary parables, graphic investigative reports, and impassioned commentaries is that it makes no sense to speak of "proper" or "improper" dreams, "virtuous" or "evil" dreams. What dreamers conjure up is what is already there before them. Hyperbole may give reality an edge; it does not invent it. Metaphor my endow fact with character; it does not corrupt it. Instead, dreams telegraph a host of emotions, they disinter buried memories, reawaken repressed cravings, rouse a lust for inaccessible pinnacles and a fondness for preposterous hopes. Staged against eerie backdrops, spoken in arcane idioms, dreams challenge reality, defy the status quo, and rise against unbending beliefs. Dreamers react to anxiety, pain, anger, and despair by surrendering to a few milliseconds of cathartic escapism and excruciating lucidity—or hours of conscious but uncontrolled contemplation. Because dreaming disconnects them, even briefly, from the conformist mediocrity of the non-dreaming mainstream (a granfalloon also referred to as "society,") dreamers are often cast as radicals, apostates, and agitators.

The tyranny of the majority isn't a threat in fascist America today. As in any Mafia state, tyranny of the minority is. A growing phalanx of phony flag-wavers in high places is poised to overpower dreamers. Our anarchic stance is at odds with the aims of the *vaterland*, which is to keep the herd in check by granting it illusory rights, and to send sacrificial lambs to slaughter when special interests decide a little war of "pacification" or "democratization" is overdue. To ensure that "society," this amorphous and self-perpetuating agglutination of private interests submits to the whims of minority rule, dreamers will be steadily enjoined to indulge in "righteous" dreams (read tame, insipid dreams) or dreams "consistent with the traditional values, attitudes, and objectives of the ruling class" (read obsequious, nauseatingly insipid and, above all, nontoxic to the powers that be).

Dreamers are free sprits caught up in eccentric and open-ended scenarios inspired by the bewildering ugliness, cruelty, cupidity, deceit, and injustice they witness while awake and stirring. Their quirky irreverence inspires fear; they are loathed by those who reject any concept or ideation that does not harmonize with their model of reality, conventions, and creeds. Dreamers remind them of what they can never be: free.

Iconoclastic, satirical, sometimes somber, my musings have always counseled against absolutism and blind faith, often with ferocious, always unrepentant, irreverence. They also warn against a new breed of scoundrels. No, they're not fugitives from justice, escapees from mental institutions, or sociopaths feeding uncontrollable grudges. Cloaked in vestments of self-granted sovereignty, they're afflicted with another kind of folly. Bent on refashioning humankind by the light of their unaided reason, they have sanctified the art of deceit by honing the science of dreambusting. They will stop at nothing to silence those who stand in their way. They will incarcerate people — or kill them — for their opinions, their beliefs (or lack thereof), their race, their caste. Quarries of choice include the naïve, the unschooled, the destitute and, increasingly, the dissenters, the headstrong, the defiant, the outspoken, the dreamers who rise up against the despotism and moral decay of their tormentors.

♦

The "Stygian depths" to which Morpheus alluded on page 7 ("the paradoxes, aberrations, deceptions, and monstrosities that define man and mark the human condition") which he asked me to reconnoiter as I stirred from a dream-laden slumber are more cavernous, gloomier, infinitely more menacing than the most terrifying hallucination that Ovid's god of nightmares, Morpheus' brother Phobetor, could have inspired. I was only able to skim the surface. Younger, bolder exorcists will venture deeper and flush out the hideous fiends they chance upon along the way.

Morpheus' pledge to deliver the innocent and the righteous from the traumas of reality and grant them serene slumber is admirable but imaginable only in the fantasy-shrouded regions of mythology or among ascetics whose renunciatory ideals lead to a joyful indifference to pleasure and pain. Attaining *ataraxia,* loosely described as a state of imperturbability, calmness, or serenity, is a universal longing. It is also a fool's errand, especially in materialistic societies or among the multitudes of innocent and righteous souls whose lives are touched, sidetracked, or compromised by nature's fury, by the miserliness, cruel apathy, and stupidity of their peers, and by the madness and sadism of their masters and commanders.

Defeating demagoguery, crushing the despotism of senseless beliefs, and dismantling the mind-manipulation machine of the capitalist ecosystem is the quixotic stuff that air castles are made of. The dreams in which creators and discoverers seek and find inspiration, those that the voiceless and the castaways pin their hopes on, are filled with wildly gyrating windmills. Reality is cunning and pitiless. Whatever the cost, false prophets who, to rule, curtail basic freedoms, shirk the law, lie, ridicule scholarship, mock the learned, defy nature, and ensnare men's souls by appealing to their worst instincts threaten the greater good and must be neutralized.

I tried. It's your dream now.

Born in Paris, W. E. Gutman is a retired journalist, a former staff writer
at the late-great New York City-based
futurist monthly magazine, *OMNI*,
the co-founder of a now defunct military intelligence journal, and the past
U.S. editor of a Russian scientific and
cultural magazine. He reported from
Central America from 1994 to 2006,
focusing on politics and human
rights. He has published hundreds of
articles, news analyses and editorials
and is the author of eleven books. He
lives with his wife in Florida.